SUCCESS
SECRETS
of the
BIBLE

JOHN EDMUND HAGGAI

HARVEST HOUSE PUBLISHERS
EUGENE, OREGON

Unless otherwise indicated, all Scripture quotations are from the New King James Version. Copyright © 1982 by Thomas Nelson, Inc. Used by permission. All rights reserved.

Verses marked NIV are taken from the Holy Bible, New International Version®, NIV®. Copyright © 1973, 1978, 1984, 2011, by Biblica, Inc.™ Used by permission of Zondervan. All rights reserved worldwide. www.zondervan.com

Verses marked ESV are from The Holy Bible, English Standard Version, copyright © 2001 by Crossway Bibles, a division of Good News Publishers. Used by permission. All rights reserved.

Verses marked KJV are taken from the King James Version of the Bible.

Cover by Dugan Design Group, Bloomington, Minnesota

Cover photo © Hemera / Thinkstock

SUCCESS SECRETS OF THE BIBLE
Copyright © 2013 by John Edmund Haggai
Published by Harvest House Publishers
Eugene, Oregon 97402
www.harvesthousepublishers.com

Library of Congress Cataloging-in-Publication Data
    Haggai, John Edmund.
    Success secrets of the Bible / John Edmund Haggai.
        p. cm.
    ISBN 978-0-7369-4729-9 (pbk.)
    ISBN 978-0-7369-4730-5 (eBook)
    1. Success—Religious aspects—Christianity. 2. Success—Biblical teaching. I. Title.
    BV4598.3.H35 2013
    650.1—dc23

                                                            2012026069

All rights reserved. No part of this publication may be reproduced, stored in a retrieval system, or transmitted in any form or by any means—electronic, mechanical, digital, photocopy, recording, or any other—except for brief quotations in printed reviews, without the prior permission of the publisher.

Printed in the United States of America

        12 13 14 15 16 17 18 19 20 / BP-CD / 10 9 8 7 6 5 4 3 2 1

I dedicate this book to the faculty members of Haggai Institute worldwide, including faculty members at the international, Middle Eastern, Mandarin (Chinese), regional, and national seminars. Each one of them has demonstrated the kind of success of which we read in Joshua 1:8:

> This Book of the Law shall not depart from your mouth, but you shall meditate in it day and night, that you may observe to do according to all that is written in it. For then you will make your way prosperous, and then you will have good success.

Collectively, these faculty members have influenced millions (you read that right, millions) to achieve true success in the 184 nations where the alumni live and work.

God has used these leaders to transform their own societies, and they personify that which they teach. They focus all their efforts on the target: presenting the gospel without compromise and without offense. They are indeed populating heaven, and only eternity will reveal the full impact of God's victories through them.

Many of the alumni have written to me to say these faculty members gave life and reality to the alumni's opportunities to transform their culture. These alumni represent every rank of intellectuality, every echelon of lifestyle, and every kind of leadership vocation. They include government leaders (from mayors to heads of state), Supreme Court justices, physicians and surgeons, media moguls (both print and electronic), university presidents and professors, authors, multinational business leaders, urban planners, financiers, engineers, manufacturers, bankers…in all, they represent 115 different professions!

They are impacting the world. The names of some appeared in a *Time* magazine list of the 100 most influential people in the world.

One lady, a prominent socialite in the Philippines, told me with tears in her eyes that it took the training at Haggai Institute under these superb and sterling lecturers to put fire and meaning in her life. She said, "I feel twenty years younger, and I'm looking to the future with indescribable anticipation." She later became one of our faculty members.

Words fail me in my effort to express the profound gratitude I feel for these marvelous people to whom I dedicate this book. Their lives and their achievements beggar description.

CONTENTS

Why the Bible Holds the Secrets of Success

> This Book of the Law shall not depart from your
> mouth, but you shall meditate in it day and night, that
> you may observe to do according to all that is written
> in it. For then you will make your way prosperous, and
> then you will have good success (Joshua 1:8).

God promises success to all those who follow this formula, to all who focus on the teachings of God's Word—"this Book of the Law." To all those who make the Word of God the subject matter of their talk (both to others and to themselves) and who meditate and observe to *do* according to all that is written, success is guaranteed.

The word "meditate" means much more than contemplation. The idea is that one should reflect on God's Word in a thoughtful way, applying its truths to every facet of life.

> Blessed is the man
> Who walks not in the counsel of the ungodly,
>> Nor stands in the path of sinners,
>> Nor sits in the seat of the scornful;
> But his delight is in the law of the LORD,
>> And in His law he meditates day and night
>>> (Psalm 1:1-2).

The success promised by God carries His own guarantee. The success may not surface immediately, but surface it will.

Folks would not have considered Jesus a success in the hours before His crucifixion. The cross appeared to put a sudden end to His life. However, after the cross came the resurrection. The number of Christians in the world today stands at 2.1 billion, compared with perhaps 200 followers on the day Jesus died.

Jesus said, "In the world you shall have tribulation: but be of good cheer, I have overcome the world."

As an example of one man's success as a result of pursuing success God's way, consider pioneer missionary Adoniram Judson.

> When Judson began his mission in Burma [now called Myanmar], he set a goal of translating the Bible and founding a church of 100 members before his death. When he died, he left the Bible, 100 churches, and over 8,000 believers. In large part due to his influence, Myanmar has the third-largest number of Baptists worldwide, behind the United States and India...
>
> Each July, Baptist churches in Myanmar celebrate "Judson Day," commemorating his arrival as a missionary. Inside the campus of Yangon University is Judson Church, named in his honor, and in 1920, Judson College, named in his honor, merged into Rangoon College, which has since been renamed Yangon University.
>
> Judson compiled the first ever Burmese-English dictionary. The English-Burmese half was interrupted by his death and completed by missionary E.A. Steven. Every dictionary and grammar written in Burma in the last two centuries has been based on ones originally created by Judson. Judson "became a symbol of the preeminence of Bible translation for protestant missionaries."[1]

In the 1950s, Burma's Buddhist Prime Minister U Nu told the Burma Christian counsel, "Oh no, a new translation is not necessary. Judson's captures the language and idiom of Burmese perfectly and is very clear and understandable."[2] His translation remains the most popular version today in Myanmar.[3]

At least 36 Baptist churches in the United States are named after Judson, as is Judson University in Illinois. Judson College in Alabama is named after his wife, Ann. Though he became a Baptist, he is honored with a Feast Day on the liturgical calendar of the Episcopal Church (USA) on April 12. In World War II, the liberty ship *SS Adoniram Judson* was named in his honor.

I think I have made my case regarding his success.

Follow the advice of this world, and you may achieve your 15 minutes of fame. But only by following the teaching or path of God's Word in the Bible will you change your life and the lives of those you know.

CHAPTER 1

The World Says "Don't Look Foolish"

The Bible Says "Know Where You're Headed"

I NEED YOU TO BE HONEST WITH YOURSELF.

If you're not prepared to confront your weaknesses and deal with them, you might as well stop reading this book right now. Plain and simple, you just don't have what it takes to succeed. You could save the time you're spending flipping through these pages.

If you *are* going to be honest, start by answering this question: If doing the right thing could injure your reputation, subject you to ridicule, or bring censure from others, would you do it anyway?

I'm asking that question because the road to success involves some tough decisions. It involves actions that other people—including your friends and family—may find hard to swallow.

So you have a choice. Either you cave in and do what everybody else does or you chart your own course because you know what you want to achieve.

That's the first secret to success you'll find in the Bible, and not surprisingly it comes right at the beginning, in the book of Genesis.

Read the story of Noah in Genesis 6–9. When Noah turned his hand to shipbuilding, people must have thought he had lost his mind. He lacked any conceivable qualification, he lived 100 miles from open water, and nothing in the current meteorological situation justified what he was doing. His project looked like madness.

And yet he kept working on an ark for 120 years.

> By faith Noah, being divinely warned of things not yet
> seen, moved with godly fear, prepared an ark for the
> saving of his household, by which he condemned the
> world and became heir of the righteousness which is
> according to faith (Hebrews 11:7).

Setting the Tone Doesn't Always Make You Popular

Fast-forward to Elijah in the book of 1 Kings.

Elijah put his reputation on the line with Israel's King Ahab.
Elijah told the king, "As the LORD God of Israel lives, before whom
I stand, there shall not be dew nor rain these years, except at my
word" (17:1).

Ahab probably thought Elijah was a deranged lunatic. And
public opinion would no doubt have been on Ahab's side.

But the next morning there was no dew, and down in the val-
leys no fog was rising. Month after month, not a cloud could be
seen. The bubbling spring on the hillside disappeared. The little
brook that formerly rippled over the rocks and down the moun-
tainside vanished. Eventually a wail could be heard in the land. As
a result of no rain, a famine was creeping up like a serpent.

That didn't make life any easier for Elijah.

Now the corrupt king began to take notice. Ahab determined
to find the man who had predicted the famine. He searched high
and low. He went to the surrounding nations and took an oath
from them that they had not hidden away this man.

By the second year the people were doubtlessly emigrating by
caravans from that God-forsaken and desolate country. In the
third year there was still neither dew nor rain. Six months later,
Ahab and his chief of staff, Obadiah, went in opposite directions,
scouring the country for Elijah.

Catch the picture. Imagine the desolation on all sides: bones of
animals bleaching, streams dried up, vegetation gone, thirst and
hunger everywhere, funeral processions bearing away the dead,

pestilence and famine and ruin and desolation from one end of the land to the other.

Obadiah finally found Elijah, and trembling like a leaf in the autumn wind, he told Elijah that Ahab would kill him if he dared go back without Elijah in his custody. Obadiah had been a courageous man. When Jezebel was killing God's leaders, Obadiah hid them by fifties in a cave. So Elijah went with Obadiah.

When Ahab saw Elijah he said, "Is that you, O troubler of Israel?" (18:17).

Elijah shot back that it wasn't he, but Ahab himself who had troubled the Israelites by causing them to forsake the commandments of the Lord and follow the pagan god Baal. In effect, Elijah said to the king, "I'm not the problem; you're the problem." Talk about fearlessness! He accused King Ahab of bringing ruin upon the country. He might as well have said, "I warned you this would happen."

Then he made a proposition. He told Ahab to arrange a camp meeting on the top of Mount Carmel. "Gather all Israel to me on Mount Carmel, the four hundred and fifty prophets of Baal, and the four hundred prophets of Asherah, who eat at Jezebel's table" (18:19).

When everyone had assembled, Elijah said, "How long will you falter between two opinions? If the LORD is God, follow him; but if Baal, follow him" (18:21). Elijah then challenged the people to lay a sacrifice on an altar and call on their god, Baal, to send fire to consume the sacrifice. And so they did.

The 850 false prophets prayed. They danced and even sliced their flesh to get Baal's attention. Nothing happened. No fire consumed their offering. Elijah taunted them, asking if Baal had maybe taken an afternoon nap and couldn't hear them. Finally, exhausted, they gave up.

Then Elijah repaired the altar of the Lord, which had been broken down. He placed the sacrifice on the altar, and to make his point absolutely clear, he also instructed the men to pour water on the wood, which they did. He told them to do it a second time and then a third time, and they did. The water filled the trench Elijah had dug around the altar.

Then in response to Elijah's 63-word prayer to the God of Abraham, Isaac, and Israel, the fire of the Lord fell and consumed the sacrifice, the wood, the stones and dust, and even the water in the trench.

This was when Elijah predicted rain. He did this with gusto, telling Ahab that he heard "the sound of abundance of rain" (18:41).

Elijah then sat on the top of the mountain, bowed down on the ground, put his face between his knees, and told his servant to go look toward the sea for a cloud.

Six times the servant came back and reported nothing. The seventh time he came back and said, "There is a cloud, as small as a man's hand, rising out of the sea!" (18:44).

Many twenty-first-century investors say, "The trend is your friend." What trend did Elijah see? Sun, sun, and more sun, followed by one very small, distant cloud. What would you project from that? What would be the safe bet on which to premise your planning and your future security?

Elijah had God's express promise of rain. And he *acted* on the promise! He *prayed*.

The clouds grew dark. Elijah warned Ahab to hurry to Jezreel to get ahead of the storm. (An aside: Elijah was a physical powerhouse. He ran in front of the chariot the 13 miles from Carmel to Jezreel!)

Both Noah and Elijah chose not to follow the current trend. They went very seriously off-road. They were in territory where even a four-wheel drive would do them no good.

Why? Because the vision that drove them wasn't the kind of vision that shows you what's right in front of your nose. It was a vision of God-empowered possibility. They could have bowed out, but they didn't. Instead, they decided to take the risk of obeying God's command.

Each man took immediate action on the vision. No procrastination. No waiting for a more convenient time. No trend watching and hedging. They saw and they acted.

The Biblical Dynamic of a Vision

In my book *The Influential Leader,* I have written at length about vision. "Vision" is the word the Bible uses for a central, durable, foundational plan. A vision prevents you from drifting. It keeps an organization together and on track. Solomon, the wisest man of all time, said, "Where there is no vision, the people perish" (Proverbs 29:18 KJV).

The Hebrew word translated "perish" could also be translated "cast off restraint." No activity in business or anywhere else will succeed unless there is a vision to draw together the effort and motivation and loyalty of the people involved. Without that rock-solid foundation, the personnel will become fragmented, critical, and sometimes destructive.

The Old Testament leader Nehemiah had a vision for a protective wall around the city of Jerusalem. He took a leave of absence from the Persian king's service and traveled to Jerusalem, where he encountered insufferable obstacles, ridicule, and attempted sabotage. Nevertheless, thanks to the strength of his vision, we read the great words, "So the wall was finished" (Nehemiah 6:15).

It takes determination.

Charles Spurgeon, the most famous clergyman of the nineteenth century, admonished his students in London to move ahead with "the blind eye and the deaf ear." In other words, don't hear anything that will derail you from your commitment to the vision. And don't see anything that will likewise neutralize your vision and diminish your effectiveness.

Follow Joshua's advice: "Do not turn from it to the right hand or to the left, that you may prosper wherever you go" (Joshua 1:7). Proverbs 3:5-6 gives similar advice:

> Trust in the LORD with all your heart,
> And lean not on your own understanding;
> In all your ways acknowledge Him,
> And He shall direct your paths.

How Do You Know What You Want?

Michael Rozak spent many years with a public relations firm in New York. He got tired of the rat race and retired to Brattleboro, Vermont, where he started brokering businesses.

He would not sell a business to anybody until they had written at least 50 pages of what they wanted to do with the business. Some would get to a half a page and say, "That's it." He would force them to keep writing.

Who will man the business? How will the doors stay open if your key person gets sick? Are you going to be open on holidays, and if so, which ones? What kind of retirement program will you provide for your employees?

He found that until he forced people to dig down deep into their subconscious and into their viscera, they were not ready to do business. He sold 103 businesses; 102 of them prospered beyond the owners' wildest dreams. One failed.

That one failed, Rozak said, because he was in the Northwest at a wedding and was not able to look over the person's shoulder to make sure he kept writing.

As the old saying goes, "How do I know what I think until I read what I wrote?" If you can capture your vision in words, you will more easily and effectively communicate that vision to other people.

During the life of the apostle Paul, only about three percent of the world's population was literate. How would he reach the most people? He could not visit them all, so he wrote. But who could read his letters? Obviously he focused on the leaders, the literati—those who could read.

His vision permitted no delay and no compromise with anything less than the preaching of the gospel to the whole world.

Writing has been the essential ingredient, the basic element in carrying out the vision. According to philosopher Francis Bacon, "Reading maketh a full man; conference a ready man; and writing an exact man."

So often I hear people say, "I know what I want to say, but I can't express it." If you can't express it, you don't know what you want to say. Dr. Robert Walker, one of the great writing coaches of all time, said, "If you can think it, you can write it. If you can't write it, you haven't thought it."

In his book *Greatness,* Steven Hayward compares the lives of two of the twentieth century's most noted political leaders, Ronald Reagan and Winston Churchill. At first sight, they were very different men. Churchill was an intellectual whose early life was shaped by his experience as a war correspondent in South Africa. Reagan went into politics from Hollywood and was often underestimated as a result. In fact, he liked it that way.

But both Churchill and Reagan wrote. Churchill's many books, historical and autobiographical, probably totaled 10 million words. Reagan wrote out completely the 320 speeches he delivered during his political career. That compares with 18 written by President Obama (at the time of this writing), whom many have considered one of the great communicators.

Churchill and Reagan made an impact with their words that was both memorable and controversial.

Churchill's radio speeches are credited with holding the British nation together in the darkest days of World War II. Yet in the aftermath of the war, when he delivered his "Iron Curtain" speech in Missouri in 1946, even fellow conservatives trashed him.

Similarly, when Ronald Reagan first referred to the Soviet Union as the Evil Empire, some of his closest friends, including political pundit George Will, went on record to disagree. Even Reagan's wife, Nancy, did not like it. But when Reagan was convinced that something was right, he did it. Period. Full stop.

Today the world lauds both men for the very speeches their friends and colleagues lambasted. They grasped what was going on at a time when most of their contemporaries still had their gaze fixed on the past. These men shaped the geopolitics of the day. They knew what they wanted to achieve.

The Rocking Chair and Ottoman

When others criticize you, staying true to your objectives isn't easy. You can easily start to doubt whether you have the qualities required to get through.

I used to be a pastor, and during the early years of my ministry I suffered indescribable stomach upset prior to preaching. The condition was so severe, the doctor prescribed medicine to keep me calm enough to make it through the message.

Like so many people who refuse to face the facts, I rationalized. After all, I had suffered severe speech handicaps. My voice was so high and raucous as a boy, my father asked me to be quiet while he was studying because my voice went through the house like a saw blade. I had a noticeable impediment until my late teens.

Now I was 22. I had studied under two of America's premier voice coaches. At the university I had won an award for oratory. In debate I had done well. Nevertheless, the fear of not performing lingered on. The old fears erupted every time I moved toward the pulpit.

At the end of every message I went home dejected, convinced that my sermon had been a bomb. For months on end, every Sunday afternoon I planned to resign the following week.

My father visited me one Sunday and sensed my distress. The following day he purchased an ottoman for me.

He said, "John, I want you to make a habit of sitting in your high-back rocking chair with your feet on this ottoman after you return from your morning service. If you're downcast, ask yourself if it's because you had not properly prepared your message. If you had prepared, then ask the Lord to forgive you for your fear and to deliver you from it. As the Scriptures say, 'Be of good courage.'"

Great advice! And it worked. Ten years later at the age of 32, I was honored to address 10,000 Christian leaders at Kiel Auditorium in St. Louis, Missouri. My message was reported in newspapers across America, including the *New York Times* and *Los Angeles Examiner*.

Since then God has granted me the opportunity of speaking in Asian cathedrals, at the Kiwanis international convention, among parliamentarians in London's Church House Westminster, to the religious newspaper editors of America, to the Society of Industrial Real Estate Brokers, to 125 CEOs of Korea's largest corporations, at a symposium of leaders representing India's ten major religions, and to an audience of 165,000 at the Maramon Convention in Kerala, India.

In the 66 years that have followed my father's sage advice, I have consciously worked on my communication skills. Even today I work on keeping my voice strong.

The Difference Between Can and Can't

Of all the high-achieving men and women I have been privileged to meet, the late Robert G. LeTourneau ranks near the top.

Though not a highly schooled man, LeTourneau pioneered the development of heavy earth-moving machinery. His machines represented nearly 70 percent of the earth-moving equipment and engineering vehicles used during World War II. He authored nearly 300 patents.

Assisted by his wife, Evelyn, he founded LeTourneau University, a private Christian university in Longview, Texas.

He was a devoted Christian and generous philanthropist. He lived on 10 percent of his income and gave 90 percent to Christian causes. Across the world, both Christians and non-Christians identified him as "God's businessman."

He had little interest in traditional education. In fact, he left school with the blessing but apprehension of his parents. He got a job apprenticing to an ironmonger in Portland, Oregon. While working in the foundry, he was given a course from an international correspondence school. He studied mechanics using these materials but never completed any course assignments. He then moved to San Francisco and worked at a power plant, where he learned welding and became familiar with the application of electricity.

He then moved to Stockton, California, and worked a number of jobs, including woodcutter, farmhand, miner, and carpenter's laborer. This knowledge of the manual trades became valuable later in life.

In 1911 the Superior Garage in Stockton hired the 23-year-old LeTourneau. There he learned vehicle mechanics. Shortly thereafter he became half-owner of the business.

The military disqualified him because of permanent neck injuries sustained in a car-racing accident. He worked as a maintenance assistant at the Mare Island Naval Shipyard, where he improved his welding skill and received training as an electrical machinist.

After the war he returned to Stockton to discover that the Superior Garage business had failed. He took a job repairing a Holt Manufacturing Company crawler-tractor. The tractor owner then employed him to level 40 acres using the tractor and a towed scraper.

This type of work captivated his interest. In 1920, at age 32, he bought a used Holt tractor, rented a scraper, and became a regrading contractor.

The next year he bought a plot of land and established an

engineering workshop, where he designed and manufactured several types of scrapers. As he combined contracting and earth-moving equipment manufacturing, his business expanded. In 1929 he incorporated his business in California as "R.G. LeTourneau, Inc."

In the 1920s and early 1930s he completed numerous earth-moving projects, including the Boulder Highway to Hoover Dam in Nevada and the Marysville Levees, Orange County Dam, and Newhall Cutoff in California.

In 1933 at age 45 he retired from contracting to devote his time and energies to manufacturing earth-moving equipment.[1]

There's much more to this remarkable story, but I want you to stop for a few moments and reflect on what you have read.

What made LeTourneau different? As you can see, only after several changes of position did he identify what he really wanted to do. But once he had caught that vision, he couldn't be separated from it. He would say, "The only difference between 'can' and 'can't' is 't.'"

From 1957 to 1968, when I was a campaign evangelist, LeTourneau often gave his Christian testimony on Saturday nights. He held crowds spellbound. Only heaven will reveal how many were motivated by his testimony to mount their fears and attempt things they previously thought impossible.

Despite dropping out of school, LeTourneau racked up a list of outstanding achievements:

- He pioneered heavy earth-moving equipment.

- He designed and built machines using technology that was years and sometimes decades ahead of its time, including the use of low pressure, heavy-duty rubber tires, two-wheeled tractor units (the Tournapull), the electric wheel drive, and mobile offshore drilling platforms.

- He built factories that supplied 70 percent of all the heavy earth-moving equipment used by Allied forces during World War II.

- He founded a university.

- He received more than 30 awards related to engineering, manufacturing, and the development of heavy equipment.

- He was presented with the Appreciation of Service Achievement 1931–1935 by Six Companies Incorporated for supplying earth-moving equipment to the Boulder Dam project.

- He was presented with the Beavers Award at the third annual awards dinner of the Beavers, an association of leaders in the heavy construction industry.

- He launched a development project in Liberia with the goals of colonization, land development, livestock introduction, evangelism, and philanthropic activities.

- He accomplished a similar project in Peru.

- He received the Frank P. Brown Medal in 1956 from the Franklin Institute, one of the oldest centers of science education and development in the United States.

- He held many respected positions throughout his life as a Christian layman, including lay leader in the Christian Missionary and Alliance Church, president of the Christian Business Men's Committee, and president of the Gideons International.

- Despite his heavy schedule, he traveled thousands of miles to attend weekly Christian speaking engagements.

I'm sure you have noticed that his achievements were often without precedent. Talk about thinking outside the box—LeTourneau rarely thought *inside* the box.

In 1953, at age 65, LeTourneau sold his entire earth-moving equipment line to the Westinghouse Air Brake Company. He had to sign a no-compete agreement, which was to be in force for five years. The Westinghouse leaders evidently believed he would be no threat at retirement age. They didn't know Robert G. LeTourneau.

As soon as he sold the company, he applied his ingenuity to the development of an electric wheel drive. In 1958, at age 70, he reentered the earth-moving equipment manufacturing business. He now offered contractors a range of high-capacity earth-moving, transportation, and material handling machines based on the revolutionary electric wheel drive system he had developed.

In 1963 his wife, Evelyn, invited me to their home for a quiet 75th birthday celebration for Mr. LeTourneau. In the middle of the meal he received a phone call from longtime friend and legendary industrialist Henry J. Kaiser, then 85 years old. I could hear only one side of the conversation but soon started cracking up with laughter. After LeTourneau hung up, he filled me in on details I could not hear.

Kaiser asked LeTourneau to help him build the Hawaiian Hilton Village. LeTourneau responded that he could not because he was busy helping Dr. Albert Schweitzer clear out the jungles in Liberia!

Single-Minded, Not Double-Minded

Two thousand years ago, James, the half-brother of Jesus, wrote this:

> If any of you lacks wisdom, let him ask of God, who gives to all liberally and without reproach, and it will

be given to him. But let him ask in faith, with no doubting, for he who doubts is like a wave of the sea driven and tossed by the wind. For let not that man suppose that he will receive anything from the Lord; he is a double-minded man, unstable in all his ways (James 1:5-8).

It's as relevant today as it was back then.

Multibillionaire Richard M. (Rich) DeVos started a company with a friend from school days, Jay Van Andel. They began the business in the basement of Jay's home. They encountered obstacles, potential lawsuits, and the opposition of governments, but they never lost sight of the vision. Nor did they veer from it in their actions.

Today, their company, Amway, which Forbes listed as the 32nd largest privately owned American company in 2010, grosses $10 billion annually in sales. And they keep growing despite the global economic downturn.

Similarly, Cecil Day had a vision for a budget luxury motel chain. In the middle of his journey to his determined destination, the 1974–1975 oil embargo hit the USA. Traffic came nearly to a standstill on the interstate highways where he was building his chain. Liquidity dried up. He was stuck with 15 percent construction loans even though many of his motels had advanced to the place where a nine percent conventional loan was justified.

Cecil Day didn't deviate from his plan. Instead, he visited three bankers daily for 21 months until he secured the lifeline he needed. By the time he died in 1978, Days Inn Hotels was one of the largest motel-hotel chains in the world.[2]

Start on any new endeavor, and you won't lack critics to tell you how likely it is you'll fail. Any enterprise requires concentrated effort and single-mindedness of a kind outsiders often don't understand.

Time to Decide

Success begins with you. Thousands, probably millions, have great ideas and high ambitions. Yet they come to nothing because they don't have the single-minded determination to realize their goals. In many cases, they are less motivated by their own vision than they are by the shifting opinions of those around them.

Outside pressure, often from those you love and trust, can kill your achievement on the starting blocks. In its multiple voices, the world will say to you, "Don't take the risk of doing something unpopular or failing and looking like a fool."

The Bible says, "Know where you're headed."

The world or the Bible—which are you going to listen to?

CHAPTER 2

The World Says "Rely on Yourself"

The Bible Says "Attract a Winning Team"

IMAGINE BUILDING A BOAT in a desert for 120 years.

That takes some self-belief. It takes some thick skin against criticism and ridicule. It takes a willingness to put your reputation very firmly on the line.

People who know what they want to achieve are almost inevitably driven to reach their goals. The intensity of their grasp on a future reality will brook no compromise. They will often see themselves as alone at the front. And all too often they are.

But they will never succeed if they stay that way. Anyone who is going to turn ambition into real success must be able to communicate that ambition to others—to turn it into a shared objective. In short, the leader must also be a visionary.

Biblical Visionaries

You need to grasp right away that not all of the great figures of the Bible had this trait.

The Old Testament prophets, for example, often felt like Isaiah, "a voice of one crying in the wilderness." They proclaimed the hard truth to a generation that refused to listen. Consequently they were marginalized and often ignored.

Consider Elijah. You will have noticed more than a little

showmanship in his duel with the prophets of Baal. All of that pouring water on the wood of the sacrifice reminds us of the escape artist who gets the attention of his audience by showing off the powerful chains and padlocks that encase him.

But for all this showmanship, and in spite of the dramatic victory that followed it, Elijah seemed unable to win the ears of those around him. Shortly after the contest on Mount Carmel, we find him hiding away in a trough of depression, asking God to take his life.

Elijah was a prophet, but he wasn't a visionary.

By contrast, Noah's monumental feat of shipbuilding could not have been achieved single-handedly. He needed men with technical skills he did not possess. He needed materials. Genesis 6:9 describes Noah as a just man who walked with God and was blameless in his time; he is not described as a master shipbuilder.

Unlike Elijah, Noah was surrounded by a large extended family. People lived a long time before the flood. The genealogy in Genesis 5 lists the age of each of Noah's ancestors—both when their first sons were born and when they died. Methuselah (Noah's grandfather) died in the year the flood started. Lamech (Noah's father) died five years before that. So the extended family would have been huge.

Perhaps the workers Noah engaged were there for the money and nothing more. But family members would not have supported him unless he had been able to sell them on his vision. Somehow, Noah must have persuaded at least some of them to turn his personal God-given goal into a family project. He needed their backing. He probably needed their cash.

Enlisting help isn't always easy. Those who work with you must be firmly convinced not only that you need their help but also that you will cooperate with them even as you want them to cooperate with you.

Genesis 14 tells the story of the kidnapping of Lot. In response,

Abraham overtook the kings who had abducted Lot. He could not have done it alone. His rescue mission required the cooperation of his 318 trained servants.

Moses never could have accomplished the emancipation of the Jewish people from Egypt without the assistance of his brother Aaron.

Solomon, the wisest man of all time, said, "Two are better than one" (Ecclesiastes 4:9). Similarly, Leviticus 26:8 tells us, "Five of you shall chase a hundred, and a hundred of you shall put ten thousand to flight."

"If I Had a Million Dollars…"

In 1890, Dr. Frank W. Gunsaulus, an educator before he became the pastor of the Plymouth Church in Chicago, preached a sermon titled "If I Had a Million Dollars."

Mr. Philip D. Armour, founder of the meat-packing company Armour & Company, listened intently to his pastor talk about the need for a technological university. His pastor said that if he had a million dollars, that's what he would create.

After the service, Armour said to his pastor, "I believe what you said. Come to my office tomorrow morning and I will give you a check for one million dollars." That's $24,300,000 in today's dollars.

There is always plenty of capital for those who can create practical plans for using it. But Dr. Gunsaulus would not have been able to establish a university without Philip Danforth Armour.

In the same way, the apostle Paul always had someone traveling with him—Barnabas, Silas, or Timothy. Paul, who was the greatest spiritual influencer of all time, Jesus Himself excepted, could never have accomplished alone what he achieved through the cooperation of other people.

Likewise we read in Luke 10:1 that Jesus Himself sent His followers out two by two. He never sent them solo.

Let's get past the rather obvious point that a group of people working together can achieve more than a single individual. The real issue is what's happening inside that group to make the cooperation happen. How does the visionary interact with those who share the vision?

Other people don't provide their services, money, and enthusiastic support for free. If you want to lead others to pursue a vision, you must maintain harmony with the people you need in order to accomplish your goal. And that harmony must include something of value in it for them.

I and We

As soon as you use the word "we," you unleash a force of unstoppable power.

In short, the whole is greater than the sum of its parts. Philosophers, business people, and politicians have affirmed this truth since the dawn of history. Caesar's armies wrote it across the face of ancient Europe. The apostle Paul spelled it out in his letters to the church.

Today, management experts impress on us again and again that what two individuals achieve separately can be achieved faster, better, and more enjoyably if those two individuals work together. You invest your influence into the lives of others to quickly and efficiently attain common objectives of mutual desire and benefit.

That's why the Bible describes Christians as "God's fellow workers" (1 Corinthians 3:9). The body as a whole can achieve benefits the individual members can never realize alone.

But the key is harmony, or unity of purpose. The cooperation of others with the same mindset and the same desired goal increases the impact exponentially.

Moses had the brainpower, the vision, and the mission, but he could not speak well. Aaron, his brother, apparently enjoyed fluency of expression.

After Paul's conversion, Christians distrusted him. They looked on his sudden change of heart as a ruse. After all, he had previously persecuted Christians. But Barnabas, one of the wealthiest Christians of New Testament times, vouched for Paul. Had it not been for that synergy, at least 13 books of the New Testament would have never been written. The greatest influence for Christ in the first century never would have been realized.

Barnabas may not have shared Paul's keenness of mind, but he had largeness of spirit. Together they combined to form a team with super intelligence and super compassion.

What Paul accomplished staggers the imagination. He traveled mostly by foot or by boat as far as western Europe, taking the gospel to people who were oblivious to the possibility of salvation.

I compute that some of these trips, even by boat, took as long as 60 days. At each place he stopped, he recruited others to assist him in his mission.

Seek Out the Can-Do People

When Paul admonished the Corinthians to be careful of the influence of their environment, he quoted an ancient Greek poet, Menander, who wrote, "Evil company corrupts good habits."

You must make the practice of focus a habit—an *ironclad* habit. You dream of it at night, and you think of it by day.

I can't give you chapter and verse for the following statement, but I know it to be true (and so do you): We tend to attract to ourselves those people, conditions, and events compatible with our state of mind.

Have you noticed that the complainers tend to gravitate toward each other? So do the successful people! Is that not correct?

I believe God has put something in the universe, maybe in the very ether of the universe, by which we attract to ourselves people, situations, and responses that reflect our own state of mind. Take every opportunity to create the kind of environment compatible with your desire.

Make sure you associate with can-do people rather than can't-do people. Be polite to everyone, but do not associate intimately with those whose thoughts and lives would wreck your own if you were to adopt their style and habits.

The Master Mind

Dr. Napoleon Hill became famous in the twentieth century for his book *Think and Grow Rich*. Then he wrote a series of other books. Later he developed the science of personal achievement.

I knew him well and spoke with him often about what he called the Master Mind. He defined the Master Mind as the mind "developed by the harmonious cooperation of two or more people who ally themselves for the purpose of accomplishing a given task." Master Mind groups exist wherever people interact to pool their intellectual resources.

America's Founding Fathers constituted a Master Mind. So did the members of the Manhattan Project, who worked under a cloak of secrecy to develop the atomic bomb during World War II. Alexander the Great had a Master Mind group of advisors more than 300 years before Christ.

Probably the largest Master Mind group ever to have existed was created by Bill Wilson and Dr. Bob Watson. These two men founded an organization in Akron, Ohio, in 1935 that now consists of more than 105,000 groups, including 2562 groups in correctional facilities in the United States and Canada. It is called Alcoholics Anonymous.

AA meets the criteria of the consummate Master Mind group. They observe a set of 12 guidelines and start every meeting with a concise statement:

> Alcoholics Anonymous is a fellowship of men and women who share their experience, strength and hope with each other that they may solve their common problem and help others to recover from alcoholism...

> Our primary purpose is to stay sober and help other
> alcoholics to achieve sobriety.

Would you agree that this group focuses on and works toward
a common goal? They meet in local groups that range from as few
as four or five in some areas to several hundred in larger cities. They
gather together at least once a week in churches, meeting rooms,
or members' homes, where they tell of their experience—how they
drank, how they came to discover AA, and how the program has
helped them. Just sharing their stories generates strength.

Bill Wilson and Dr. Watson adapted many of their ideas and
their 12 steps from another Master Mind called the Oxford Group,
formed in 1919.

The Leather Apron Club

Benjamin Franklin organized a club of young workmen in the
fall of 1727. Often called the Leather Apron Club, it also went by
the appellation Junto.

It was not drawn from the social elite. A small group of enter-
prising tradesmen and artisans made up the membership. Nevertheless they had self-respect and ambition and fancied themselves
gentlemen.

Every member of the Junto helped the others succeed. They
recommended books, shopkeepers, and friends to each other.
They fostered personal development through discussions on top-
ics related to philosophy, morals, economics, and politics. They
met for four decades and eventually became the American Philo-
sophical Society.

Here's how Franklin portrayed the Junto in his *Autobiography*:

> I should have mentioned before, that, in the autumn
> of the preceding year [1727], I had form'd most of my
> ingenious acquaintance into a club of mutual improve-
> ment, which we called the Junto; we met on Friday
> evenings. The rules that I drew up required that every

member, in his turn, should produce one or more queries on any point of Morals, Politics, or Natural Philosophy [physics], to be discuss'd by the company; and once in three months produce and read an essay of his own writing, on any subject he pleased. Our debates were to be under the direction of a president, and to be conducted in the sincere spirit of inquiry after truth, without fondness for dispute, or desire of victory; and, to prevent warmth, all expressions of positiveness in opinions, or direct contradiction, were after some time made contraband, and prohibited under small pecuniary penalties.

The effects of the original Junto are still evident today. The Junto gave us our first library and volunteer fire departments, the first public hospital, police departments, paved streets, and also the University of Pennsylvania.

Ponder the last sentence in Franklin's quote. Acrimony, rancor, and negativity have no place in a group committed to productivity and excellence.

A similar spirit of cooperation typified the Chicago Big Six. This group of six Chicagoans merged friendship and expertise in the early 1920s. Here's the roster:

- Andrew Carnegie (probably the main motivator)
- William Wrigley Jr. (of Wrigley chewing gum fame)
- John R. Thompson (owner of a chain of lunch rooms)
- Albert Lasker (owner of Lord and Thomas ad agency, then the largest in the world)
- Charles A. McCullough (owner of the Parmalee Express Company)
- John D. Hertz and William C. Ritchie (owners of the Yellow Cab Company)

At that time, the combined annual income of the Big Six was estimated to be $25 million. In today's dollars, that could be close to $4 billion.

Not one member of this group had an advanced education or started out with financial advantages. All were self-made men. They made their fortunes without personal start-up capital and without extensive credit. They formed a group solely to get feedback on their ideas.

The Secret of Harmony

To use the biblical line of the apostle Paul, "As much as depends on you, live peaceably with all men" (Romans 12:18).

"Can two walk together unless they are agreed?" (Amos 3:3). The unequivocal answer jumps at you, doesn't it? Of course, the answer is no.

Napoleon Hill wrote, "You cannot enjoy outstanding success in life without power, and you can never enjoy power without sufficient personality to influence other people to cooperate with you in a spirit of harmony."[1] To which I would add only one qualification: "…to cooperate with you in a spirit of harmony *toward a positive goal that benefits those you influence.*"

He also reminds us that a "pleasing personality is the 'fulcrum' on which you must place the 'crow-bar' of your efforts, and when so placed, with intelligence, it will enable you to remove mountains of obstacles. This one lesson…will teach you how to transform your personality so that you may adapt yourself to any environment, or to any other personality, in such a manner that you may easily dominate."[2]

The "Impossible" Task

In 1964 I received a vision to impact the world.

I had been a pastor of four churches. I had preached at convocations large and small across America and around the world—in small buildings, in magnificent cathedrals, and to 160,000 people in Kerala, South India. But this vision focused on a new concept of taking the gospel of Jesus Christ to the entire world.

It troubled me that the people around the world who knew about Coca-Cola far outnumbered those who knew about Jesus Christ. Candidly, Coca-Cola had done a far superior job marketing their products than Christians had done in strategically presenting the gospel "for salvation to the ends of the earth" (Acts 13:47).

Yet which was the greater task? I did not for one moment believe that Jesus commissioned me and those of one mind with me to failure. Nor did He mock us with an impossible assignment in creating Haggai Institute.

To obey this vision and its correlate mission meant that we would...

- bring together the top leadership of each of the non-Western nations

- prioritize attention and effort in those nations where the gospel was barely known

- enlist a blue-ribbon non-Western faculty

- bring the Christian leaders of those nations to a non-Western locale for specialized training in advanced leadership for effective evangelism

Nothing less would achieve this goal.

To fulfill this vision required the best faculty available—men (and later women) who had demonstrated a transforming influence in their own local environments. It also meant they must create their own teaching materials. In the West, we are given to syllogistic thinking: the major premise, the minor premise, the conclusion. In the East, and indeed in most other parts of the world, people communicate not in Greco-Roman thought forms but rather with allegories, parables, and stories.

Furthermore, the people selected for the faculty must have such stellar reputations that their very names would attract interest and respect.

And as I insisted, the training must be done in a non-Western locale. It would be self-defeating for those leaders to return to their nations with a "made in America" label on their backs.

It took until September of 1969—almost five years—to put all the elements in place.

During that time, I enlisted the involvement of the first man in history to build a megachurch, Dr. Kyung-Chik Han of Seoul, Korea. From an original nucleus of only 27 refugees from North Korea, he had built the Young Nak Presbyterian Church to 60,000 members. He did it all with local funds.

Korea, at that time, was one of the poorest nations in the world. Some areas in India, Indonesia, and elsewhere may have had less income, but the survival needs were not as great. Korea had rough weather. The people needed more clothing and fuel for heat in the wintertime.

What Dr. Han accomplished stands as unique and unequalled in its achievement for the glory of God.

Another man, Dr. Ernest Watson, put his enormous global reputation on the line for an experiment that many thought was foolhardy. He also served as dean of our faculty.

Along the way came Dr. Won Sul Lee, the president of Hannam University in Korea and the secretary general of the International Association of University Presidents. He had received his PhD in diplomatic history from Case Western Reserve University in Cleveland, Ohio.

Not long afterward the faculty was strengthened by the addition of Fr. Dr. Anthony D'Souza, who established two major leadership institutions in India—the latest, the Xavier Institute of Management. This man, a Jesuit, has served for years as the personal representative of the pope. He conducts the orientation of the new bishops every September in Rome.

Then there was Dr. Benjamin Moraes, who built the dynamic Copacabana Presbyterian Church in Rio de Janeiro. He also wrote the penal code for the nation of Brazil. He could read, write, and speak 12 languages. He led 54 international missions.

I could fill this book with names, credits, and successes of the people who came together in founding Haggai Institute. The point is, I never could have done it alone.

I did have certain advantages. I'm an ethnic Syrian, which gave me a unique acceptability in Asia. But without these stellar luminaries, we never would have gotten off the ground.

As I write this, more than 86,600 men and women have completed their advanced training in leadership for evangelism at Haggai Institute for Advanced Leadership. They work in 184 nations.

The leaders agree, before acceptance, to transfer the training to at least 100 of their peers within two years after returning to their home nations.

The alumni include chief justices, surgeons, physicians and hospital directors, media moguls, multinational businessmen, urban planners, university presidents, authors, manufacturers, and political leaders, including heads of state—in short, the kind of people who lead in their nations.

I repeat: This never could have been realized had it not been for the synergy created by those of like mind. You will find it absolutely essential to bring together those who thoroughly understand your vision and agree with it wholeheartedly.

The Other Gates

John D. Rockefeller and his advisor, Baptist minister Frederick Gates, moved in perfect synergy. Yet they could not have been more different. Rockefeller was enigmatic, patient, and taciturn. Gates was operatic, impetuous, and outspoken.

Gates was a force of nature. All the historians of the Rockefellers have been fascinated by Gates and discuss at length his character and influence on the family. Although Rockefeller first hired Gates to provide shrewd counsel on his philanthropy, he soon enlisted Gates's help in business.

In 1917, when a journalist asked Rockefeller to name the greatest businessman he had ever encountered, Rockefeller overlooked the many dynamos he had met throughout his long career (including Carnegie, Flagler, and Ford) and named Gates.

He said of Gates, "He combines business skill and philanthropic aptitude to a higher degree than any other man I've ever known."[3]

Gates could never have achieved what he did or risen to the heights to which he ascended had it not been for Rockefeller. And Rockefeller could never have accomplished what he did without Gates.

In fact, some credit Gates with being the instrument in turning Rockefeller's deteriorating health around at 54 by suggesting he engage the bulk of his time in philanthropy.

Rockefeller took synergy seriously.

He placed a premium on internal harmony and tried to reconcile his contending chieftains.

A laconic man, he liked to canvas everyone's opinion before expressing his own and then often crafted a compromise to maintain cohesion. He was always careful to couch his decisions as suggestions or questions. Even in the early days, he had lunch daily with his brother William, Edward Hartness, Henry Flagler, and Oliver Payne to thrash out problems.

As the organization grew, he continued to operate by consensus, taking no major initiative opposed by board members. All ideas had to meet the supreme test of unanimous approval among strong-minded men.

Even Rockefeller wasn't a team of one.

Time to Decide

Being a visionary isn't just about having a clear and driving goal. It's also about attracting others into a program so you have the means to achieve that goal.

That may take some effort. Hot tempers must be subdued. Manipulation and selfishness must be curbed. You must demonstrate graciousness of spirit, willingness to serve, and a passion to help. In short, you must have a pleasing personality.

For many high achievers, that's hard work. But if you want to succeed, you've got to be able to do it. The world will tell you that if you want a job done properly you should do it yourself because nobody else is going to perform to your exacting standards. The message of the Bible says: Attract a winning team. Find the quality people who can grasp your vision and help you deliver on it.

The world or the Bible—which are you going to listen to?

CHAPTER 3

The World Says "Grab Your Opportunities"
The Bible Says "Check the GPS"

IN 1918, DR. EMORY S. BOGARDUS of the University of Southern California wrote a book called *Essentials of Social Psychology* in which he describes "the focalization of psychic energy."

I may have read that chapter 30 times. It reminds me of the apostle Paul's testimony: "One thing I do" (Philippians 3:13).

In the 21st century, we suffer from a surfeit of opportunities—to buy products, to get involved in associations and communities, to divide our time between leisure activities, to read, listen, watch, play, and surf the Internet. To change our residence, job, appearance, beliefs.

But the serious follower of the Lord Jesus does not follow any distraction that keeps his life goal from influencing him.

His thermostat is set. His barometer remains steady. He does not move to alternate proposals like a weather vane in a windstorm—mentally, emotionally, or spiritually—even if those proposals emanate from the mouth or pen of dedicated Christians.

They don't know the divine will for his life.

The true follower of the Lord Jesus keeps his or her eyes on Jesus and Jesus alone, "looking unto Jesus, the author and finisher of our faith" (Hebrews 12:2). When Peter, James, and John saw Moses and Elijah on the Mount of Transfiguration with Jesus, a cloud overshadowed them. God spoke out of the cloud, and they fell on their faces.

Here's the pivotal message: "When they had lifted up their eyes, they saw no one but Jesus only" (Matthew 17:8).

The serious believer knows the ultimate objective of the life that the Holy Spirit has mapped out for him or her. The believer must spend each moment "in the zone"—in the current day. He or she must ruthlessly annihilate every distraction.

You may define a distraction as anything that diverts your attention from the day's objective. After all, the day's objective is a component of the life objective the Holy Spirit has mapped out. That's the same Holy Spirit whom the Lord Jesus promised "will guide you into all truth" (John 16:13).

So How Do You Find a New Direction

Getting the fundamentals right allows you to make all the other "downstream" decisions.

Let me tell you more about the origins of my life's work with the ministry that came to be known as Haggai Institute. When I started it, I had been working as a pastor and evangelist. The new venture was a dramatic departure from anything I'd done before. I had felt so strongly about the pastorate—on what basis did I justify such a profound change?

The answer is that starting the new ministry didn't change any of the fundamentals. It was a decision about methods, not about aims. Let me explain.

I like to organize projects. God has surrounded me with highly competent people, and I'm confident we could have substantially enlarged the impact of my existing evangelistic ministry. But there was a problem.

In the early 1960s I detected an imbalance of witness between the Western nations and the non-Western. Western nations were sending missionaries overseas, often at great expense, but not making great strides in evangelism.

A visit to western Asia in 1964 convinced me that new methods must be discovered and employed if the gospel of Christ was to reach the peoples of the non-Western world—which was the largest part of the non-Christian world.

It was obvious to me that trained national Christian leaders were the ones to penetrate their own areas with the gospel. The West was losing acceptability because of the growing nationalism in the emerging nations, which was often associated with resentment against Western paternalism, whether real or imagined.

Originally I had no intention of getting into this ministry myself. Three factors, however, intensified my motivation for evangelizing the non-Western world.

The first was that I found no church group or organization providing the training I felt necessary to meet the needs of the church outside the West.

Second, during 1965 and 1966, spiritually perceptive people (missionaries from the West as well as leaders from the East) expressed concern over the subtle shift in world mood and the concomitant requirement to change mission strategy.

The third factor was the 1966 World Congress on Evangelism in Berlin, which, to me, highlighted the wasteful duplication and overlap in some areas of missionary work and shocking gaps in other areas.

In 1968, at the behest of Indonesian leaders, I led an evangelistic effort in Jakarta, Indonesia. It was the first time in Indonesian history when Pentecostals and Presbyterians, the two largest groups in that country, cooperated along with the other denominational groups. But effective as this effort was, the largest impact of all was the Indonesian people's influence on me.

I met many leaders who asked questions about my methods

as an evangelist. As a result I conducted a brief seminar for them on the "how" of evangelism, and that seminar reinforced the idea born during my 1964 visit to western Asia.

At first, because I wasn't sure, I sheltered the idea in secrecy. I like to weigh new potentials carefully, sifting and exploring them. But as others have wisely said, nothing can withstand the force of an idea whose time has come. Thus in the autumn of the following year, we announced a seminar in Switzerland, inviting credentialed leaders from several emerging world nations.

Of that seminar, men like Roland J. Payne from Liberia, holder of two academic doctorates and later the Lutheran bishop, said, "I will never forget the ministry and witness we encountered in Switzerland. What you started here should have been started twenty years ago."

I was both elated and perturbed. Enthusiasm for missionary endeavor has long been on the wane in North America. Christian publishers, for example, shy away from books with overseas settings or themes. Americans at times have a frighteningly narrow view of the world and the mission of the church.

Missionaries have done a great job in every corner of the globe. But they've had to learn by mistakes as well as by success. One of the mistakes—a very big mistake—has been the effort by missionaries to bring Asians, for example, to a Western understanding of Christianity rather than presenting the gospel in an Asian context.

I thank God for the traditional Western missionary, because I am a second-generation product of that movement. Presbyterian missionaries took the gospel to Damascus, Syria, in the late nineteenth century. My father's uncle came to know Christ as his personal Savior and Lord. He, in turn, won my father to faith in Christ.

So the decision to start the ministry that became Haggai Institute followed naturally—one might even say unavoidably—from the beliefs I had always held as a pastor and evangelist. Winning the world for Christ demanded a new methodology, not a new message.

Saying No—Even to Money

If I had wanted to change direction completely, I could have done so on several occasions.

In 1959, when I was 35 years old, Napoleon Hill came to Louisville, Kentucky, and offered me the complete ownership and control of the Science of Personal Achievement Course he had produced. He asked for only a modest royalty. I declined.

It floored him. He could not understand why I would decline. He said, "You'll make more money in one year than you will make the rest of your life as a pastor of a church."

He was right. But, as I told him, I enjoyed some invisible perks he did not understand.

It grieved me to turn him down. He was a dear friend. And he honestly wanted not only to promote his concepts but also to help me.

Along the way you'll have to stand firm to your convictions. That will require you to surround yourself with people whose thoughts harmonize with yours.

The Power of Influence

This kind of focus on your core vision saves you from unnecessary distractions and increases your chances of success. It does so because all your effort is directed in exactly the same direction.

It's a little like felling a tree with an axe. The more accurate you are, the less scattered the blows, the more quickly you will bring the tree down. A person of normal mental and physical ability may, by deliberate concentration of energy, attain superior levels of achievement.

The biographer of Oliver Wendell Holmes, one of America's most famous jurists, said that "from the moment Holmes entered law school, he never once scattered his fire."[1] He made every action—writing, speaking, teaching, adjudicating—the product of considered and concentrated attention.

The famous Dutch-born American editor and Pulitzer Prize–winning author Edward Bok said that "concentration means success."[2]

He served as editor of the *Ladies' Home Journal* for 30 years. He coined the phrase "living room" as the room of the house that previously was most commonly called the parlor or drawing room. In his definition of success, he did not emphasize genius or talent, but only concentration and focus. He believed that by this process one can do an ordinary thing extraordinarily well.

Columbus sailed an ordinary boat, but he secured an extraordinary result.

John Wanamaker sold ordinary dry goods, but he sold them extraordinarily well.

Ignacy Paderewski played well-known musical compositions (as well as his own), but his interpretation of them produced an extraordinary result.

Benjamin Franklin flew an ordinary kite, but he made an extraordinary observation. Incidentally, Franklin earned a well-deserved reputation for industry and thrift. He said he was inspired by the verse in Proverbs 22:29: "Seest thou a man diligent in his business? He shall stand before kings; he shall not stand before mean men" (KJV). He said he considered industry a means of obtaining wealth and distinction. And he concentrated on industry and thrift.

You cannot explain that kind of focused attention apart from dedication to a life-compelling purpose. You need the tenacity of a bulldog, the capacity for incessant work, and an unswerving pursuit of your life goal.

The apostle Paul, one of the supreme intellects of all time, suffered indescribable persecution. But this was his response:

> None of these things move me; nor do I count my life
> dear to myself, so that I may finish my race with joy,
> and the ministry which I received from the Lord Jesus,
> to testify to the gospel of the grace of God (Acts 20:24).

In *The History of the Decline and Fall of the Roman Empire*, Edward Gibbon claimed—and many historians and political scientists have agreed with him—that the influence of the apostle Paul contributed to the decline and fall of the corrupt Roman Empire. Paul lived for two years in his own rented quarters in Rome. During that time he preached the gospel without surcease, and many of "Caesar's household," a term referring to what we would call today the civil service, professed faith in Christ.

Neither his enemies' attacks nor his friends' efforts to moderate his plans moved the dauntless apostle from his single focus.

Control What Influences You

When you concentrate your attention, you activate the powerful law of self-talk (also known as self-suggestion or autosuggestion). This moves into your subconscious, the source of your beliefs. Only what you put into your mind consciously—or what others put in it—will condition it. And remember—others can influence your mind without talking to you.

Before you take exception to that last statement, think for a moment. Perhaps you have phoned a friend with whom you haven't spoken for months. The minute the friend hears your voice, she says, "I was just picking up the phone to give you a call!"

Or consider a husband and wife traveling in a car without talking for an extended period of time. All of a sudden each starts talking—saying the same thing. How do you account for that? Whether we understand it or not, transference of thought occurs.

This is one reason why you must constantly and consistently repeat in your words and in your thoughts the object of your desire. Never lose that focus.

That's what makes it so important that you spend time each day in Bible study and prayer, preferably the first thing upon awaking, so as to beneficially condition the subconscious.

Remember, every word you hear, every sight you see, and every other impression you receive through any of your senses influences your thought.

In addition to Scripture, you will want to read materials that strengthen your focus (preferably books rather than magazines or ephemeral publications).

I am so committed to this truth that it influences the clothes I wear, the house in which I live, the car I drive, and the arrangement of my home office.

Focus can enhance your income, expand your influence socially, and increase your efficiency in every area of your life.

Focus requires self-control, which is one aspect of the fruit of the Holy Spirit (Galatians 5:23). God is the source of that fruit, but that does not mean we are to do nothing. God provides the air, but you must breathe. God provides the peristalsis, but you must chew the food. God provides the water, but you must drink. God provides "every good gift and every perfect gift" (James 1:17), but you must act.

I have suggested to family and friends that they limit the amount of time spent watching newscasts. For one thing, many are laced with inaccuracy; not every newscast is news. Much of it is editorializing.

Do everything in your power to enlist your spouse in your thoughts and plans. Include your spouse in all new strategies.

Henry Ford and Thomas Edison achieved what they otherwise could not have done because of the strong women who believed in them and encouraged them. When Mrs. Edison was asked to identify her husband's chief trait, she said, "Concentration!"

Master the discipline of focusing on a given target at will for whatever length of time you desire. (This is really the character quality of self-control.) When you have mastered this, you have learned the secret to achievement greater than you ever dreamed possible.

A Lesson from Qufu

I don't want anything of a material nature I don't already have—with one exception: access to a private jet capable of transporting me in minimal time to any spot in the world. (As of this writing I have completed 103 around-the-world trips in addition to many intercontinental trips.)

Recently I was invited to take part in the anniversary of Confucius in Qufu, China.

I normally get up between four thirty and five thirty in the morning. The first commercial flight out of our airport toward the Orient did not depart until three in the afternoon. That meant I could not depart until ten hours after awaking.

The first leg—to Tokyo—would have taken 13 hours. After a two-and-a-half-hour layover, I would take a three-hour flight to Shanghai, where I would wait again before proceeding to Qufu. By the time I could have gone to bed, 37 hours would have elapsed.

With a private jet, I would awaken, shower and dress, eat breakfast, drive to a nearby private airport, and it's wheels up at eight o'clock.

In nine hours, I would touch down in Helsinki, Finland. There I would have a fine meal, a good room, and eight hours of sound sleep. The flight from Helsinki to my destination in China would be seven hours!

If my time is worth anything, and as the Lord's work requires our best, I need access to a private jet.

I would never permit Haggai Institute to purchase or lease a jet even if it had the money. It would bring about understandable criticism. So my focus is how to generate the funds personally to secure this kind of travel.

I have to believe that what I am doing is more important than the political activities of Nancy Pelosi, the celebrity activities of Barbra Streisand, or even the corporate activities of company executives who understandably need the convenience and efficiency of private jet travel.

Further, when folks travel with me, we can engage in productive thinking and planning and debriefing. Commercial flights don't permit that incalculable advantage.

I have continued my focus on this for some time, and I believe I will have this commodity very soon. And it *is* a commodity.

Humanly speaking, I wouldn't care if I never made another trip. I've been there, seen it all, and done a great deal. However, one cannot lead an army from behind a desk.

Now, in focusing, I bring several senses into play. For instance, I can visualize the jet just coming out of the hangar. I visualize the interior as I approach the seat I will take. I hear the loud roar of the jet engines. I feel the desk that I pull over to work on. I also feel the leather of the chair in which I am seated. I hear the click of the left armrest as I raise it to proper position. I hear the click of the seatbelt as I fasten it.

I see the cockpit personnel, and I hear them as they give last-minute instructions. I mentally taste the food I'm about to eat and smell the coffee I'm about to drink. All five of my senses come into play. This sharpens my focus. I visualize the desire as an accomplished reality.

I don't want to own a private jet. I only want to have funds to lease whatever jet is necessary for a given journey. And I'm also visualizing Wi-Fi on board so I can use Skype and other Web-based applications while in flight.

I believe this dream and fervent prayer will have been realized by the time you read this chapter!

Focus is the key.

A friend said, "It's so expensive." I agreed. Then I asked, "Do you consider me an irresponsible spendthrift for driving an Audi?"

"Of course not. Besides, you keep your automobiles for many years."

I said, "Compare the cost of my car with that of John Wesley's horse. Is the ratio between my car and the private jet any greater than Wesley's horse and my car?"

"I had never thought of it in that way. You're right."

Time to Decide

Life throws opportunities your way. It's not always obvious which are worth pursuing. Using opportunities requires you to focus on your life plan. Focus that is founded on your key life goals will deliver you from the capriciousness of conventional thinking and changing fads.

When you are faced with big decisions about the future, the world says to you, "Grab your opportunities. After all, even if you don't feel 100 percent committed to an offer, you may decide to take it anyway because it might be a long time before something else comes over the horizon."

By contrast, the Bible says, "Check the GPS." In other words, God has designed a map for your future, and finding your place on the map will guide you into the right path. Better to pause than to take a wrong turn.

The world or the Bible—which are you going to listen to?

CHAPTER 4

The World Says "Know Your Limitations"
The Bible Says "Ditch the Word 'Impossible'"

SUPPOSE YOU'RE IN A HOSPITAL operating room awaiting surgery. The nurse has just given you a sedative before the full anesthesia. Suddenly you catch sight of the surgeon. He's in the corner of the room, wringing his hands.

His face registers agony. His body language exudes great distress. You hear him quietly moaning, "Oh, I don't know why I took on this responsibility. I'm just not up to it. I hope I can get through it."

In all probability you would shake off the sedative and bolt out of the room!

No one wants to be cut open by a surgeon who lacks confidence. That surgeon has the necessary training—now he just needs to believe in his ability to perform his duty. He needs confidence.

So do you.

A friend said to me, "How can I have confidence in the midst of all the problems that engulf me?"

I told him that confidence in God is the foundation of effective living to His glory. The Bible warns us against putting confidence in the wrong things.

Hebrews 10:35 says, "Do not cast away your confidence, which has great reward." The apostle Paul gives us a great example of this kind of confidence when he writes in Philippians 4:13, "I can do all things through Christ who strengthens me." A more literal translation is even better: "I am almighty in the One who continually keeps pouring His power in me."

Here Paul makes an unequivocal statement of confidence. He already revealed it in Philippians 3:4-9. If anyone had reason to be self-confident, he writes, it was he. After all, he was...

- circumcised on the eighth day,
- of the stock of Israel,
- of the tribe of Benjamin,
- a Hebrew of Hebrews;
- concerning the law, a Pharisee;
- concerning zeal, persecuting the church;
- concerning the righteousness which is in the law, blameless.

Then Paul follows up with this amazing statement:

> But what things were gain to me, these I have counted loss for Christ. Yet indeed I also count all things loss for the excellence of the knowledge of Christ Jesus my Lord, for whom I have suffered the loss of all things, and count them as rubbish, that I may gain Christ and be found in Him, not having my own righteousness, which is from the law, but that which is through faith in Christ, the righteousness which is from God by faith.

When You Can't, You Can

Paul didn't write these words from Philippians in the air-conditioned comfort of an apartment atop one of Rome's famed seven hills. No, Paul was in prison. By today's standards we would consider the Mamertine Prison inhumane. Unlike modern penal institutions, it did not have peppermint-striped sheets, color television, and fitness centers.

The Romans had banished Paul to a dreaded dark cell. Being kept alive in conditions like these was considered a greater and more humiliating punishment than death. Here those who had been sentenced to death awaited execution. Sometimes when a governor desired to gain a political advantage, he detained prisoners there for a long time.

Paul could have whined, "How can I accomplish anything here? Surely, the Lord knows that I am immobilized by my imprisonment."

Yet instead, through all this, Paul said, "I am almighty."

What Were Paul's Limitations?

We know that the apostle could not study his beloved books and parchments. We know that his son in the faith, Timothy, could not visit him in his imprisonment.

Nevertheless, Paul spoke with joyous confidence: "Rejoice in the Lord always. Again I will say, rejoice!" (4:4).

He said, "Be anxious for nothing, but in everything by prayer and supplication, with thanksgiving, let your requests be made known to God" (4:6).

Compared to this, the child of God has no justification for complaint—ever—regardless of how blistering the circumstances or how intolerable the environment.

Knockout Confidence

Paul said, "I am almighty." If he had stopped after these three words, he would have dishonored the Lord, insulted the people to whom he wrote, and written an unvarnished falsehood.

But he adds the moderating phrase that makes his first

statement absolutely correct: "I am almighty in the One who continually keeps pouring His power in me."

As a child, I was small and sickly. I was the prey of every bully on the school playground. One day during a holiday in Grand Rapids, Michigan, in the summer of 1934, I enjoyed the company of my cousin, Alex Haddad.

I had accompanied him down to Seymour Square to pick up some groceries for his mother. We had nearly returned to their little house on Burton Street when three big guys in a pickup truck came by and shouted, "Haddad, get yourself and that @(#*% Hebrew, Wop, Dago cousin of yours out of here before we mop up the gutter with you."

Immediately I cringed. I thought to myself, "Uh-oh, here comes another beating." Then I looked over at Alex, and my fears subsided; a peaceful calm replaced them. In fact, I started to smile.

That year, Alex was the AAU wrestling champion in the 175-pound division. At 15, he was much a man. His biceps were like cannonballs, and his pectoral muscles looked like bronze marble slabs. But strangely, Alex did not answer back.

I said, "Alex, you're not going to let them get by with that, are you?"

He replied, "You know what the Bible says. If they hit you on one cheek, turn the other."

I had never remembered Alex being that spiritual before, but I was in no position to argue, so I kept walking with him toward the house. We went inside the little picket fence, and just as we got to the front door, he handed his bag of groceries to me and said, "Take these in to Mom, okay? Tell her I forgot something; I'll be right back."

I knew exactly what he had forgotten. I shoved the groceries inside the front door and trailed him back down to Seymour Square.

He surmised that the insulting roughnecks were on their way to Miller's ice cream parlor. I got to the location just in time to watch Alex knock one of the three guys out cold and addle a second with another powerful punch while the third ran away in stark terror.

I pushed back the shoulders of my four-foot-ten frame, brushed the palms of my hands together, and said to myself, "Anyone else?"

What had converted me from a terrified little boy to a calm and serene person of positive optimism? Simply this: Alex was near.

The apostle Paul knew the source of his power. Sitting in prison, he knew the Lord was near.

Living in that awareness brings about a behavioral change that cannot be explained in human terms. It's often the only major difference between a defeated Christian and a victorious Christian.

You Can If You Continue

The word "continue" comes up in the New Testament repeatedly.

Continue in God's kindness. *Continue* to work out your salvation. *Continue* in what you have learned. *Continue* in faith. *Continue* to live in Him. *Continue* in prayer. *Continue* in love. *Continue.* Continuity is the essence of the faithful child of God.

Paul sensed that God was continually pouring His power in him.

Many of us have that feeling when we are in the middle of a success seminar or a stirring church service. We feel safe and invincible. And who wouldn't?

It's the tough times that count. I'm referring to the continuity that carries you through, not only when the environment is favorable but also when the situation is excruciating.

God provided manna for the people of Israel as they made their long trek in the desert. It must have had just the perfect ingredients for optimum nutrition. They were to gather only enough for one day's supply. If they gathered more than one day's supply, it rotted and stank. The only exception was the day before the Sabbath. On that day they could collect two days' supply so they wouldn't work on the Sabbath and thus violate the commandment to remember the Sabbath to keep it holy.

When I was a boy, we sang, "Moment by moment, I'm kept in His love. Moment by moment, I have help from above." Unfortunately, in many of our churches, some of the older members think that seniority automatically produces spiritual superiority. But if you study the Bible, you will notice that some of the most glaring cases of backsliding took place in older people.

Noah was more than 500 years old when he got drunk and shamed himself before his sons. David was a grandfather when he committed adultery with Bathsheba. Josephus tells us that Peter, the same one who denied Christ three times, was the eldest of the disciples.

To continue, you need a fresh supply of biblical confidence every day. Hyperventilating for 30 minutes doesn't mean you can go the next 30 minutes without breathing. Gorging yourself for a month doesn't mean you can go the next month without eating. Continuity means pressing on day by day and hour by hour. "I am almighty in the One who continually keeps pouring His power in me."

Are you aware of this inexhaustible and continuing supply of divinely endued power? If so, are you utilizing it for success?

Do you really believe that God "is able to do exceedingly abundantly above all that we ask or think, according to the power that works in us" (Ephesians 3:20)?

Convert Your Impossibilities

God does not think in terms of limitations. Our God is a God of the impossible. Jesus said, "With God all things are possible"

(Matthew 19:26). So don't make the mistake of always playing safe and sanctimoniously thinking you're being humble. That kind of humility is simply lack of faith.

Real humility and confidence are not mutually exclusive. Indeed, they are interdependent. If I am walking in fellowship with God, I will be active in my prayer life. I will be active in my Bible study. I will be active in my witnessing, not just publicly but also personally—face-to-face. And I will be active in my financial giving!

An Arabic proverb spells out the nature of confidence. Read the words carefully.

> He who knows not, and knows not that he knows not,
> is a fool; avoid him.
> He who knows not, and knows that he knows not,
> is a student; teach him.
> He who knows, and knows not that he knows,
> is asleep; wake him.
> He who knows, and knows that he knows, is a wise
> man; follow him.

The King of Confidence

Earlier I mentioned Dr. Kyung-Chik Han.

I dedicated my early book on leadership, *Lead On!*, to Dr. Han. I consider him the greatest leader I have ever met or heard about (excepting Jesus Himself). You can only say that once.

This dear man fled from the North Korean communists. He arrived in Seoul, South Korea, penniless and with only the clothes on his back. He bore on his body the marks of the Lord Jesus.

In Seoul he established the Young Nak Presbyterian Church with only 27 refugees. He challenged them to meet with him at five every morning for prayer.

In November of 1946, the fledgling flock secured an old tent.

The snows came early that year. One Sunday morning, as they sat in the cold tent with a few inadequate stoves, the melting snow became so heavy it shredded the canvas panels of the tent, and it collapsed.

The melting snow mixed with the people's tears as they asked Dr. Han, "What are we going to do?"

Dr. Han inspired them in the strength of the Lord. "We must build a great church."

A widow walked to the front and said, "I don't have any money, but here is my wedding ring." Another lady followed and said, "I will bring my rice bowl tomorrow and the spoon. I can borrow my neighbor's and eat at different times."

Another member said, "I will bring my blanket tomorrow because my partner and I work different shifts. I can use the blanket to sleep when he is working, and he can use the blanket at the normal time."

By 1970, when I preached there for the first time, Young Nak Church possessed one of the most beautiful Gothic-structured church edifices I had visited. And the church's annual income at that time was the equivalent of more than $20 million. To my knowledge, no other church in the world received that kind of income (except one or two that had substantial television income).

Dr. Han led his members to build colleges, orphanages, homes for the elderly, and other institutions to help the helpless and hurting. And they planted 506 other churches. One was located in California, and within 20 years it was the third-largest church of any denomination in the state.

How do you explain it? Dr. Han reveled in the continuing power that the Lord Jesus poured in him, and he acted on it knowing that the Lord had promised His ability to do exceedingly abundantly more than Dr. Han could ever ask for or think.

When I hear people complaining that they don't have enough

money to do what God wants them to do, I am sickened inside. South Korea, once one of the poorest nations in the world, is now a prosperous nation with one of the highest living standards in the world. I attribute it to Dr. Han.

According to leaders in Young Nak Presbyterian church, when the North Koreans met with the South Koreans for the first time several years ago in Pyongyang, one of the first things they asked the South Koreans was "How is Reverend Han?"

Confident People Dare to Give

God requires His children to give a tithe of their "increase" (Deuteronomy 14:22). That includes not only salary and dividends but also the increased value of their assets.

> "Bring all the tithes into the storehouse, That there may be food in My house, And try me in this," Says the LORD of hosts, "If I will not open for you the windows of heaven And pour out for you such blessing That there will not be room enough to receive it" (Malachi 3:10).

So often over the course of my long life, well-meaning church members have said, "Dr. Haggai, I simply do not have enough money to tithe. When I finally get my bills paid and get out of debt, I will tithe."

That's an old saw from hell. Tragically, this lack of confidence in God's promise—and thus confidence to act boldly—robs the disobedient of the promised divine blessings.

God doesn't give us resources to squander. He doesn't give us power to ignore. He doesn't provide strength for us to snub in practice despite our high-sounding words.

I took 35 years to appreciate the insight of John H. Sammis, who wrote the hymn text "Trust and Obey."

So many people want to respond to God's saving grace with a freedom-loving lifestyle that owes nothing to anybody. Yet the one-word, all-encompassing result of salvation is *obedience*.

The Last Command

Years ago, I met one of the most remarkable couples I have ever known. Craig Wierda was 31, and his wife, Emilie, not quite 30. They captured the vision of training non-Western leaders to obey Jesus' instruction to evangelize the world.

They immediately began supporting Haggai Institute and enlisting others. Emilie persuaded her parents to come to Maui to see for themselves what the work was like. She convinced her father and mother that they should underwrite a session for $250,000— and they did.

On the way back in their private jet, Mr. Edgar Prince, Emilie's father, said, "We need to underwrite a session every year for the next three years." They have done far more than that and for far longer. Within one month after that flight home, the Lord took Ed Prince home. Mrs. Prince has continued their amazing support for more than 17 years.

Craig and Emilie Wierda brought dozens of people to see the ministry. This young couple had the vision to renovate a four-star hotel, the Maui Sun, into a five-star, state-of-the-art training center. They have put millions of dollars into this ministry, including the renovation of this facility.

Emilie told one of America's leading upscale furniture manufacturers, Mr. G.W. Haworth, about this ministry in such a compelling way that he provided the furniture at an enormous discount. In fact, he made a gift of some of the furniture and also gave money for sponsorships.

Emilie brought an architect and his colleagues all the way from Michigan to Maui for the work. They imported the finest woods. They did not want the Lord's work to be done shabbily. Many consider this center to be without equal anywhere in the world. How to explain it? Two young people acted in confidence on the knowledge that the Lord Jesus kept on pouring His power in them.

Better to Be David than Goliath

David was the youngest and smallest of eight sons of Jesse. Goliath stood nine feet six inches tall.

Goliath represented the Philistines. He mocked the Israelites and challenged them to send one of their men to fight him. King Saul stood head and shoulders above all the other Israelites, but like the rest of them, he quaked in his boots.

David, however, considered Goliath a big bully who could be felled. His exact words: "Who is this uncircumcised Philistine, that he should defy the armies of the living God?" (1 Samuel 17:26).

His oldest brother, Eliab, angrily accused David of pride and insolence. David turned to some others, but they belittled him as well and reported David's comments to King Saul. No one else was willing to take up Goliath's challenge, so Saul summoned David to come have an emergency discussion with him.

David gave Saul a brief résumé. He told Saul that God had enabled him to kill both a lion and a bear. He assured Saul that just as God had enabled him to overpower wild animals, so God would enable him to defeat Goliath.

Saul then offered David his armor, including his helmet and a coat of mail. But David replied, "I cannot walk with these, for I have not tested them" (verse 39). Instead, David took a sling and five smooth stones. With the very first stone he killed Goliath. He then unsheathed Goliath's sword and beheaded him with his own weapon.

The Philistines fled, and the Israelites prevailed.

The story has become proverbial. People who have never read the Bible are familiar with David and Goliath. Underdogs who prevail are routinely called giant-killers. But David wasn't just courageous, clever, or lucky. The book of Proverbs tells us very accurately what was going on with Goliath. "The fear of man brings a snare, but whoever trusts in the LORD shall be safe" (Proverbs 29:25).

Time to Decide

Contemporary psychiatrists have often said that one of the greatest problems facing people today is meaninglessness. What greater meaning can there be than walking in the confidence of knowing that the Lord Jesus keeps on pouring His power in us and that we have nothing to fear? We move, walk, and pray in confidence.

That confidence is not rooted in our own personality or circumstances. In fact, recognizing our own lack of ability is one of the first qualifications for success if, like Paul the apostle, we place our confidence in God. The prophet Isaiah said, "In quietness and confidence shall be your strength" (Isaiah 30:15).

A willingness to attempt the impossible is a key ingredient of success—not because impossibilities are really possibilities in disguise, but because the God in whom we place our confidence has no limitations.

The world says, "Know your limitations because that way you'll be safe."

The Bible says, "Ditch the word 'impossible' because that word is like shackles on your psyche."

The world or the Bible—which are you going to listen to?

CHAPTER 5

The World Says "Don't Mess Up"
The Bible Says "Never Waste a Failure"

I CAN SPEAK ABOUT SETBACKS from a deeply personal perspective.

Owing to the brutalizing effects of a mismanaged birth, my only son, Johnny, was confined to a wheelchair for his entire 24 years.

As time passed, my wife, Chris, and I watched him experience the stages of development. Internally, they were normal. Externally, they were abnormal. He was denied one of life's foremost assets—a sound body.

He saw us walk about the room. He saw us sit and stand and move our arms. He saw us pick up objects with our hands.

He wanted to emulate all of it. God knows how deeply it hurt to see Johnny struggle to manipulate his body. Deep in his eyes we saw a longing to stand and walk and reach out to touch and hold. Anguish made its mark in his face as, with the passing of time, he realized that the world of normal people was not to be his world. But he cherished that world.

As he grew older we took him outside, sometimes for rides in the car. More frequently Chris or her mother would push him along the sidewalk in his wheelchair. He wanted to be where people were. He sat for hours watching children play, squealing with delight at their antics, lurching his twisted little body at the sight of a baseball bat swinging, growing tense in the exciting moments of a basketball game.

Always we kept probing, searching out any possibility by which we might bring him closer to a normal life.

For example, when he was a very small child we introduced him to therapy. If you have observed children with severe disabilities, you may know about "patterning." It is a procedure in which the therapist guides the limbs of a child in the simulation of a crawl—somewhat the same as in swimming—until the child's mind adapts to the action and he is able to take over for himself. Multitudes of children who would otherwise have been immobile for life have learned at least to crawl through the patterning process.

For Johnny, patterning therapy demanded a much more extensive procedure.

To achieve any results at all, the therapist told us, Johnny would need to have five sessions a day. They could be conducted at home. However, each session required five women—a total of twenty-five each day.

The therapist loyally recruited people for us. Most women could come for just one session each week, so we had more than 100 volunteers. Still, Chris expedited much of the therapy herself.

Johnny tried hard to achieve. No athlete in Olympic competition ever tried more strenuously to win. How he struggled with resolution in his eyes!

He did learn to crawl, just a little. But patterning was of benefit beyond its specific intent. When Johnny subsequently began to develop severe osteoporosis, the doctor told us that his bones might have gone to powder without that exercise therapy.

Later we secured a costly patterning machine, which tended to manhandle Johnny rather uncomfortably. Yet he did his best to accommodate. Like us, he seemed to envision continued improvement in his physical condition. He was willing to extend any effort, however uncomfortable or painful and for whatever length of time, to achieve improvement.

"You're a real trouper, buddy!" I would tell him, and he would glow in response.

Our highest hope with patterning was that we could develop substitute nerve pathways to bypass the damaged ones so he could learn to walk. In 1965, however, after two years of fruitless striving, we decided that the procedure was doing more harm than good, and we decided to stop.

I think Johnny was relieved. And like us, he was disappointed.

But though he lacked physical ability, he showed increasing mental aptitude. Chris introduced him to as many experiences as possible. She taught him the fragrance of flowers. He seemed to have a normal sense of touch, and she let him see and feel various objects in the house. He discovered the different textures of cloth. He learned colors. He became keenly sensitive to different sounds inside the house and outside. And he amassed a huge number of friends from the surrounding neighborhood.

In the end, he lived many more years than the doctors expected. He became a prayer warrior for my ministry. Hidden inside a tragic failure was a God-given success.

Success Is Never a Straight Line

Whenever I think about failure, I remember Johnny, and suddenly I see everything in perspective. He struggled against truly overwhelming odds, and because Chris and I cared for him, we also struggled.

Through Johnny, God taught me that what looks like a failure is often a road to success that we might never have found any other way. Failure and success are always bound up together. They are two sides of the same coin.

I saw Babe Ruth play baseball in Fenway Park in Boston in

1928. He had chalked up more home runs than any other baseball player—a record that stood until Hank Aaron surpassed it in 1974. What most people forget is that he also struck out more times than any ballplayer in history.

One might say that your success is often in direct proportion to your failures.

Dr. Napoleon Hill told me about an extended visit with Thomas Edison in his home. As he recounted the story, he said he asked Mr. Edison how many times he had experimented with the electric light filament before it was a success

Edison answered that it was something like 1200 times.

Dr. Hill then asked, "Mr. Edison, how do you account for the fact that you succeeded the last time?"

Edison quipped, "I exhausted the possibilities of failure!"

Dr. Hill pressed on. "But suppose you had not succeeded— what would you have done then?"

Edison said, "I would still be experimenting instead of wasting my fool time talking to you!"

Every time Edison conducted an experiment, he wrote detailed reports in his notebooks about what he did and what the results were. Many pages in his notes are decorated in various flowery styles of handwriting. He even wrote poems. He drew many sketches. Evidently, whatever he was thinking, he wrote it down.

Failure never stopped him. He rarely became discouraged when experiments didn't work out. Each failed experiment shifted his thinking to a new direction.

He was able to solve problems and learn from failure. He saw every failure as a step on the road to success.

Legend has it that he failed 10,000 times in his experiments on storage batteries. But he said, "I have not failed. I've just found 10,000 ways that won't work."

Thomas Carlyle said that "genius is an infinite capacity for taking pains." Edison never gave up. He looked at every failure as an opportunity.

Few Succeed the First Time

In the Old Testament, Jacob fell in love with Rachel, the younger of Laban's two daughters. He asked Laban for Rachel's hand in marriage. Laban, ever the manipulator, said, "Work for me for seven years, and you can marry her."

Jacob worked for seven years. At the end of that period, the crooked Laban said, "You can't marry the younger sister when the older sister is still unmarried, so you get Leah."

Obviously, Jacob didn't like the arrangement. Reading about his temperament, I would suppose he was furious. But he worked another seven years for the love of his life, Rachel.

The sad thing about the episode was that Jacob was as conniving, scheming, and crooked as his father-in-law. With the help of his conniving mother, Jacob had stolen his brother Esau's birthright and thus the father's blessing.

Jacob had maneuvered himself into serious trouble.

Later, when Jacob learned that his brother Esau was coming to meet him, he sent an envoy to Esau with a huge gift of oxen, donkeys, flocks, and male and female servants, along with this message: "I have sent [these]…that I may find favor in your sight."

Esau appeared to ignore the bribe, because Jacob's servants returned with the news that Esau was indeed coming—with 400 men.

Fear terrorized Jacob. He arranged his family and holdings in two groups in preparation for the meeting the following day.

That night Jacob sent his family across the brook Jabbok while he tarried alone. During the night he wrestled with God, and at dawn he said, "I will not let You go unless You bless me!"

The next day, when Jacob and Esau met, they embraced and wept.

Jacob was undoubtedly one of the most successful people in history. He also ranks as one of the biggest rascals and the engineer of some abysmal failures.

I like the title of Dr. Erwin Lutzer's book *Failure: The Back Door to Success.*

Like Joseph, some of the most successful men in American industry suffered brutalizing failures before they struck success. Henry Ford, F.W. Woolworth, R.H. Macy...in fact, Macy failed seven times before his store in New York caught on.

You fell down the first time you tried to walk.

You almost drowned the first time you tried to swim.

You didn't hit the ball the first time you swung a bat.

English novelist John Creasey earned 733 rejection slips before he went on to publish 564 books.

When in Rome, "musing amidst the ruins of the Capitol," historian Edward Gibbon decided to analyze one of the greatest failures in the world. The job took him two years and produced the classic *The History of the Decline and Fall of the Roman Empire*—six volumes long and rarely surpassed in its accuracy and detail.

What Links Failure to Success?

- "Let us not grow weary while doing good, for in due season we shall reap if we do not lose heart" (Galatians 6:9).

- "The plans of the diligent lead surely to plenty, but those of everyone who is hasty, surely to poverty" (Proverbs 21:5).

- "The soul of a lazy man desires, and has nothing; but the soul of the diligent shall be made rich" (Proverbs 13:4).

- "He who has a slack hand becomes poor, but the hand of the diligent makes rich" (Proverbs 10:4).

George Bernard Shaw, the famous socialist author and playwright, wrote for nine years before a publisher accepted his writing. Everything I've read about him leads me to believe he never permitted discouragement to dissuade him from his goal.

Discouragement is a no-no for the child of God.

We began this book with the verse: "This Book of the Law shall not depart from your mouth, but you shall meditate in it day and night, that you may observe to do according to all that is written in it. For then you will make your way prosperous, and then you will have good success" (Joshua 1:8).

The Scripture also says, "Be strong and of good courage, do not fear nor be afraid of them; for the LORD your God, He is the One who goes with you" (Deuteronomy 31:6).

When 42-year-old J.K. Rowling delivered the 21-minute commencement address at Harvard University in 2008, she said that after college, she lived for seven years on welfare. Here are her words:

> Ultimately, we all have to decide for ourselves what constitutes failure, but the world is quite eager to give you a set of criteria if you let it. So I think it fair to say that by any conventional measure, a mere seven years after my graduation day, I had failed on an epic scale. An exceptionally short-lived marriage had imploded, and I was jobless, a lone parent, and as poor as it is possible to be in modern Britain, without being homeless. The fears that my parents had had for me, and that I had had for myself, had both come to pass, and by every usual standard, I was the biggest failure I knew.[1]

By the time she had been out of college 14 years, she appeared in the *Forbes* magazine list of the world's richest people. She had amassed a net worth of more than $1 billion.

When Richard DeVos cofounded Amway with his school buddy Jay Van Andel, they rented an auditorium with 200 seats to enlist people to distribute their products.

Two people showed up! They had to drive home because they didn't have enough money for a motel room for the night. Lesser men would have abandoned the idea and said, "Well, we thought it was a good idea, but it just won't work."

Not Rich or Jay. They pursued the biblical advice, "Whatever your hand finds to do, do it with all your might" (Ecclesiastes 9:10 NIV). Today, Amway grosses $10 billion annually.

You may be familiar with legendary copywriter Joe Sugarman, whom the *New York Times* dubbed the Mail Order Maverick. Sugarman said one success out of every ten projects makes him a fortune. Suppose he gave up after a string of four or five losses!

Ted Nicholas, the highest paid copywriter in history, has produced more than $7 billion in revenue. He said he made his fortune with three or four wins out of every ten efforts. Suppose he had given up after a dry run of six or seven sterile attempts!

When Benjamin Disraeli delivered his maiden speech to the British House of Commons, he was shouted down. He vowed, "Though I sit down now, the time will come when you will hear me." And hear him, they did. Forty-one years later, Disraeli had their ear and their support. He served with distinction twice as prime minister. Some consider him Britain's most scintillating leader with the exception of Winston Churchill.

Paul J. Meyer is the founder of Success Motivation International. On several occasions he has shocked his audiences by telling them that 65 percent of his businesses failed. He then told them the lessons he learned from his failures.

The Bicycle-Repairing Multibillionaire

Dr. Mochtar Riady, an ethnic Chinese Indonesian, always had

his heart set on banking. But fifty years ago, ethnic Chinese could not work in prestigious positions in Indonesia.

Stifled in his desire, he resorted to importing and selling bicycle parts. He worked fervently and faithfully and always gave the customers a square deal. Banking seemed a far-off dream—maybe an illusion—yet he maintained his focus and determination to someday go into the banking business.

Finally a bank gave him a menial job. He sustained his work ethic and continued his studies. He maintained an incredible pace until he earned a doctorate.

He then formed the now world-famous Lippo Group of companies, including Lippo Bank and later the Lippo Life Insurance Company. His multinational business also included urban development, retailing, properties, healthcare, education, and the Internet.

He bought a 600-acre shantytown, and in a period of less than three years, he and his son James developed it into a "city of tomorrow." He provided all the people in the area with better homes than they ever dreamed of. He also gave them employment opportunities previously denied to them. He built a 300-bed hospital, a five-star hotel, and housing that compared favorably with the upscale residential districts of any city on earth. Some global business analysts considered Lippo Karawaci the most advanced city in the world.

Dr. Riady made arrangements for his sons to receive the best possible academic education as well as the best possible practical education (working in financial, insurance, and property institutions). The sons developed great business capabilities, unusual acumen, and superior relational skills.

On many occasions Dr. Riady laid everything on the line and exposed himself to potential financial disaster. Through it all, he treated people fairly and ensured that they would enjoy value-added benefits by their alliance with his businesses.

Dr. Riady suffered opposition, including severe invectives and cruel betrayals. During the financial troubles in Southeast Asia, some Indonesians were angered by what they perceived to be political corruption and unleashed their hostility on Riady.

The damage to Lippo Karawaci amounted to millions of dollars. Yet I never heard any member of the family complain. Dr. Riady must have suffered profound grief when some of those whom he had emancipated from poverty vandalized and looted stores and factories in Lippo Karawaci.

During the 1990s, pundits and politicians scandalized the Riadys, accusing the Riadys of guilt by association. The Riadys did not defend themselves; they simply put their confidence in God and waited patiently for the truth to finally emerge. Dr. Riady has never allowed his environment to control him. He pressed on to his goals.

The most striking part of the Riadys' office is the magnificent artistic portrayal of Jesus washing the disciples' feet.

When I visited him in 1997, I was struck by the quiet presence of Mrs. Riady in the corner of the office as she prepared her Bible study lesson.

Dr. Riady, a convert to the Lord Jesus Christ in his mature years and after verifiable success in business, demonstrates day by day the power of converting failure into success. A less intrepid spirit would have folded on many occasions. Mochtar Riady has impacted the world positively by allowing failures to breed amazing success.

Setbacks Don't Come Much Bigger Than This

In 1964 on a visit to Beirut, Lebanon, I made a startling discovery. By then, a plethora of American businesses like Coca Cola, IBM, and Singer Sewing Company had realized the day of Western dominance in the non-Western world was over. The church had not.

Driven to act on this, I prayed and then planned an ambitious six-week seminar that would train leaders from the non-Western world to use their leadership for effective evangelism.

It wasn't cheap. I had commitments for about $85,000. I was expecting $50,000 from an oil man, $20,000 from a transportation tycoon, and $10,000 and $5,000 gifts from some others. But during the spring of 1969, the stock market plummeted. These honorable people who had promised me the money in good faith simply didn't have the cash anymore.

On September 9, 1969, my secretary, Alberta Schuler, said, "Preacher, Pan Am said they will cancel all the tickets unless they receive the money tomorrow." I hit my forehead with the palm of my hand and said, "Oh my, has the time come so quickly?"

I said to Alberta, "Please take down this cablegram: 'Due to unexpected and unavoidable obstacles, training session postponed indefinitely. Regrets, regards, prayers. John Haggai.'"

When she finished taking down the message, she looked up at me and started to cry. I said, "Don't do that. I don't need that right now."

"Why does the Lord allow this?" she asked.

"Alberta, don't blame the Lord. Blame me. Apparently I got ahead of the Lord. It's entirely possible that I misread what I thought was His leading. Pray that I will know what to do and that there will be as little damage as possible."

Then I added a curious directive that surprised even me. It was two o'clock in the afternoon. I said, "Alberta, if you don't hear from me by four o'clock, send the cable to all the people involved."

She replied, "But that's going to destroy your credibility with the lecturers and participants. And frankly, Preacher, I don't think you will ever have a training program if this one doesn't go through!"

"Alberta, all of those things and more flashed in my mind the moment you told me the problem. Now is the time to pray."

I went into my office and literally spread-eagled before the Lord. I was in agony. I asked the Lord to forgive me if I had been headstrong and had moved in a direction that was not His will.

At quarter to four, the buzzer on my phone intercom interrupted my prayer. Lying on the floor, I lifted my left hand to the desk to answer the call.

"Dr. Haggai?" Alberta's voice was soft, but I heard it.

"Yes, what is it?" I barked, with a strain in my voice that showed my impatience.

"Carl Newton of San Antonio is on the line."

"I'm sorry, I can't talk with him now. I'll call him back," I said.

"But you must talk with him," she insisted.

"I don't have to talk with him or anyone else right now—not even if it's the archangel Gabriel. I'm talking to his Boss."

But she persisted. Although I was annoyed at her, I took the call. "Hi, Carl. How can I help you?" I said.

"John," Carl replied, "the market has gone to pot. My stock has dropped from $57 a share to $13 a share since May."

I had been straining my ears all day for encouraging news like that? "I'm sorry, Carl," I said. "I've been talking to the Lord about another matter, and I'll include the problem in my prayers."

"Wait a minute, knucklehead," he said. "You need some money, don't you?"

"Of course, but you don't sound as if you're in a position to help."

"Well, John, I can't give you any stock. Since I'm CEO and a major stockholder, the divestiture of any stock by me could cause a run on the company."

"I understand, Carl."

"But wait a minute. We're able to get an 8 percent $100,000 loan for 12 months. Within this time, I should be able to arrange for some liquidity. Call the man at your bank in Atlanta. Janie and I wired a gift of $100,000 a couple of hours ago."

I could scarcely believe what I had just heard. When I hung up the phone, the clock on my desk read six minutes to four. Six minutes later, there would have been no Haggai Institute!

Later, Carl said to me, "I didn't know how I was going to do it, but I was impelled to act. I've never made a commitment I was proud of which, at the time that I made it, I could see any possibility of fulfilling."

As I write this, more than 86,600 world leaders working in 184 nations have passed their advanced training to millions of others.

I failed, and I learned from the failures. God gave success.

Time to Decide

Not everyone has experienced success, but failure strikes everyone at some time or another. Often it strikes many times. You can accept failure as final, or you can regard it as only a setback, a temporary defeat.

The world says, "Don't mess up because mistakes can damage your finances and your reputation." The Bible teaches, "Never waste a failure because failure provides a great education that can boost your chances of succeeding."

The world or the Bible—which are you going to listen to?

CHAPTER 6

The World Says "Achieve and Enjoy"
The Bible Says "Achieve and Build"

I HAD THE INSPIRING EXPERIENCE of meeting J.C. Penney in Florida in 1960. He was 85 at the time. He lived ten more years.

Penney's father, the Rev. James Cash Penney, served as an unpaid minister and farmed to make a living. He told his son and namesake, when he was only eight years old, that he must buy his own clothes. He did it to impress on his son the value of money and self-reliance.

J.C. Penney did buy his own clothes. He did it by purchasing a pig and fattening it to sell for a handsome profit. He then turned to growing and selling watermelons.

Penney graduated from Hamilton High School in 1893 but didn't have the money for higher education. With the aid of his father, he secured a position as a clerk in a local dry goods and clothing store. He started on February 4, 1895, at $25 a month.

His health began to fail two years later. On the advice of his physician he left in 1897 for Colorado to regain his health. He worked briefly at two stores and then bought a butcher shop. He chose to go bankrupt rather than donate whiskey to the cook of a local hotel in order to obtain business.

In Colorado, he latched on to an opportunity to work in T.M. Callahan's first Golden Rule Mercantile Company store.

Two years later, Callahan paid Penny $50 a month to work at his Evanston, Wyoming, store. Three years later, Penney opened a new Golden Rule store in Kemmerer, Wyoming. The store was capitalized at $6,000, of which one-third was Penney's. That made him a junior partner.

His ownership increased his ambition, excited his imagination, and gave him the idea of someday having a chain of stores of his own based on the same principle of partner-owners who shared in the profits. For many years he lived frugally in an attic room over the store. He opened the store at seven a.m., closed at nine or ten p.m., and worked half a day on Sunday.

In 1903 he acquired a one-third interest in another Golden Rule store, and a year later he supervised a third store in which he'd been sold a one-third interest. In 1907 Penney bought Callahan's remaining share of these three Golden Rule stores.

He selected and trained store managers, convinced that they had the duty to share their experience with their promising salesmen. He delegated responsibility, put his faith in his people, and eventually made them partners when new stores were opened. He shared one-third of the profits with the store managers—a motivating factor for success in business, according to Penney. Profit sharing was unknown to most businesses at that time. To embark on this practice required a tenacious belief in his own ideas. The plan found its biblical roots in the Golden Rule Callahan had named his chain after: "Do to others as you would have them do to you" (Luke 6:31 NIV).

Penney liked to be called "the man with a thousand partners." In fact, that is the title of his autobiography.

He lost $40 million (more than $500 million in today's dollars) in the Great Depression. At age 54, he had to start over again with borrowed money. He soon regained his empire. He died at age 95 with 1661 stores.

In his later years, he reflected, "I believe in adherence to the Golden Rule, faith in God, and the country." And here's the clincher. Despite his countrywide fame in business, he often said, "I would rather be known as a Christian than a merchant."

Penney was more concerned about the future than the past. His own achievements mattered less to him than the future he was building for those around him, including his employees.

Who's Going to Remember You 50 Years After You're Dead?

The Bible teaches, "None of us lives to himself, and no one dies to himself" (Romans 14:7).

The late Pitirim Sorokin, who founded the sociology department at Harvard University, said that the average person influences at least 3000 others. If that is true, then people like you who are reading this book probably influence multiples of that number.

Certain events and ideas survive because they are powerfully influential. These include the Great Depression as well as quotations from Shakespeare, Patrick Henry, and other notables throughout history.

But J.C. Penney understood that the most influential force of all is not an event or an idea. It's a person.

So what influence do you currently exert on anyone or any group of people? Will it guarantee a lasting effect? What beneficial impact will your influence have throughout the remainder of their days and throughout eternity?

You may not have heard the name John Bolten, yet his influence affects each of our lives every day. He was a German who came to this country and became father of the plastics industry. Even better, he was committed to the lordship of the Christ and had a powerful impact for good and for God on the lives of multiplied thousands of people.

When I met his son John Bolten Jr. in 1982, he could have

passed for a mixture of Anthony Eden and Douglas Fairbanks Jr. He stood over six feet tall, had an athletic build, and cut an imposing figure.

Though he was reserved in manner, his charm won the hearts even of his casual acquaintances. As a raconteur, he held audiences of one or of thousands spellbound.

He qualified as the ultimate jet-setter, a Western playboy. He divided his time between business, travel, polo, skiing, and yachting. Hubert von Pantz, in his book on Europe's leading socialites, placed John alongside such notables as Clark Gable and Gary Cooper.

Bolten was a frequent and popular guest at von Pantz's Mittersill Castle in Austria, a favorite playground of the rich, where the leading lights of the Americas laughed and danced with European aristocracy.

John felt at home in these circles and moved with ease in society's highest echelons. He attended the most prestigious gatherings of the most sought-after people.

At Mittersill in the early 1960s, John met Ines—one of Europe's top models, a raven-haired beauty whose stylish good looks turned heads wherever she went. They married in 1964. He was the socialite German, she the glamorous, engaging Italian Swiss. It marked a second marriage for him, first for her. For both of them, this was "for keeps."

They lived in the fast track. They worked and played on three continents. They appeared to have it all—wealth, respect, and popularity.

John even embraced a faith of sorts. He'd gone to a fine Christian school (strangely enough, the same one I attended, though we were separated by four years and didn't know each other). He had accepted Christ as Savior at the age of 15 and never doubted from that time onward that he would go to heaven when he died.

Yet his religion was little more than an insurance policy. "No one looking at my lifestyle could have accused me of being a Christian," he says. Faith became a matter of appearances only— something to which he paid lip service out of respect for his parents and grandparents.

Only when his father fell sick in 1982 did the truth catch up with him. John took Ines back to the family home on Via Balleria in Palm Beach. An insufferable ennui took hold of him. The artificial jet-set values had dulled the luster of the so-called good life. All his accomplishments had left him dissatisfied and worse.

In ways by which society measures success, he had pretty well swept the board—as businessman, socialite, and philanthropist. Nevertheless, in more personal and essential criteria for joy and serenity, he viewed himself as an abysmal failure.

And so it was that one evening, when his father had retired to bed, John and Ines decided not to go out partying but to spend a quiet evening together watching TV.

The Cowboy

Nothing on television caught their attention, and John was moving to switch the TV off when suddenly Ines said, "Go back to that cowboy."

John flipped back.

The cowboy was singing. Not about deer and antelope and being at home on the range, but about Jesus. This got the Boltens' attention. A cowboy singing about Jesus?

After he had sung the song, the cowboy, LaVerne Tripp, gave his testimony. He'd grown up in a poor family in West Virginia, but singing had brought him fame and fortune. Influential people in show business discovered him at 22, and his career took off like a rocket. By 28, he owned a house in California, a Mercedes, a Jaguar, and a BMW. Unfortunately, he was also drinking heavily, taking drugs, and wrecking his marriage with a series of casual affairs.

A young Christian musician in his band urged Tripp to attend a meeting every time a visiting evangelist came to town. This annoyed Tripp, but finally, just to silence the young man, he agreed to go. To his surprise, he felt an irresistible desire to return the next night to hear the evangelist again. On the third night, Tripp swallowed his pride and walked forward at the evangelist's invitation to accept Christ as Lord and Savior.

Somehow though, he couldn't gain control of his life. Once he got drunk at a party and disgraced himself. Devastated and convinced that he was too bad to be a Christian, he staggered home and pulled his pistol from the drawer, intending to commit suicide.

At that precise moment, the phone rang. It was his Christian friend. Out on a walk, the young man had just passed a telephone booth when he felt impressed to call Tripp.

"Are you all right?" he asked.

He could tell from Tripp's voice that something was very far from being all right.

The young man jumped in his car and drove straight to Tripp's house. He found the bandleader slumped over a table with the pistol still in his hand. Tripp poured out his frustrations.

The young man listened and then replied, "You've been trying to live the Christian life in your own strength. You can't do that. You must surrender. Jesus must be the Lord of everything you do. He alone can change your life."

When John Bolten heard Tripp's testimony, he dropped to his knees and sobbed.

During the tender years of his childhood, his parents forced him to attend a stern and rigid Plymouth Brethren assembly. He and his sister, Gisela, sat in the back of the auditorium feeling excluded and bored. Later, glad to leave behind the black ties and black socks, he attended Boston's Park Street Congregational Church. Never before this night at his father's Palm Beach mansion, however, had he felt such a powerful touch from the Holy Spirit.

Gradually he became aware that Ines too was sobbing. They both surrendered their lives to the lordship of Jesus Christ that evening, and a new dimension of power and victory permanently changed their lives.

The young musician invested his influence in Tripp's life. Tripp used his reputation to testify and unknowingly extended his influence to the Boltens. That is the world-changing power of the investment of influence.

What Kind of Footprint Do You Leave?

Male or female, wealthy or poor, literate or illiterate, famous or obscure…we all wield influence over others whether we know it or not. We cannot avoid it. And if we are wise, we will invest that influence as we would invest money in stocks or bonds or real estate. We will exploit to the fullest its potential for accomplishing the good.

That is, we will make sure that our influence blesses and benefits others and permanently strengthens our God-honoring work.

Since John and Ines Bolten converted, they have influenced people in more than 180 nations. And that influence grows, not just arithmetically but exponentially. They have been the instruments of winning to faith in Christ a multitude of people from every rank of intellectuality, every level of culture, and every echelon of society.

The focus must center on positive influence—not a bland influence and certainly not a negative one. And no success can ever be reached in isolation. Success always involves other people.

True, the Boltens' success story never made page one of the *New York Times* or the television evening news. Nevertheless, it works as powerfully without news releases and celebrity as with these transitory bursts of stardom.

The Bravest Believer in the New Testament

I consider John Bolten Jr. a twenty-first-century Barnabas.

> When Saul had come to Jerusalem, he tried to join the disciples; but they were all afraid of him, and did not believe that he was a disciple. But Barnabas took him and brought him to the apostles. And he declared to them how he had seen the Lord on the road, and that He had spoken to him, and how he had preached boldly at Damascus in the name of Jesus (Acts 9:26-27).

Later, after the apostles had been scattered from Jerusalem, Barnabas continued investing in Paul's life.

> Barnabas departed for Tarsus to seek Saul. And when he had found him, he brought him to Antioch. So it was that for a whole year they assembled with the church and taught a great many people. And the disciples were first called Christians in Antioch (Acts 11:25-26).

Note the subtle importance of the first verse. Barnabas is a role model of influence.

When Saul of Tarsus, the arch-persecutor of the church, was struck down and converted and came to Jerusalem to join the disciples, nobody trusted him. No one else believed he was genuine.

Yet Barnabas put his reputation on the line. With his enormous influence, he interceded for the new convert. Barnabas, perhaps the most generous man in the New Testament, took Paul to the apostles and gained a hearing. He became the influence—the channel—through which the apostles could finally hear the voice of God speaking.

Imagine the consequences if Barnabas had been unwilling to invest his influence on behalf of Saul (renamed Paul). For one thing, we would not possess 13 or 14 New Testament books (about half the total books in the New Testament) because Paul would have never written them. Without those epistles, how diminished the influence of Christianity would have been in the centuries to come.

Edward Gibbon, the classic chronicler of the Roman Empire, could not have identified Paul as a major reason for the decline of the Empire.

Through Barnabas, God made possible the whole of Christian history as we know it.

A single introduction, a single word, or a single piece of well-chosen advice can influence the entire world for good. That same gift, which we all possess, has in John Bolten Jr. been refined to a rare purity.

As few people I've known, Bolten has an overmastering passion to use his influence, his resources, his energy, his Bible study, and his prayer time to further the work of God worldwide.

Talk about influence!

The Woman Who Changed the World

You may know very little about a woman named Susanna. She bore 19 children, of whom 9 died before adulthood.

She was born 342 years ago and lived for 73 years. The times in which she lived denied her the benefit of any labor-saving devices. She owned no refrigerator or even an icebox. She had to shop several times a week because foods had no preservatives. She made her children's clothes. She had no electric iron, electric dishwasher, washing machine, or dryer.

Yet she taught each of her children Latin and Greek. Each child was proficient in both languages by the age of ten! One son, John, was teaching Greek at Oxford by the time he was 21.

There were no public schools, so Susanna personally tutored the children. She taught them to be courteous in speech, to cry softly when it was necessary to cry at all, and to subdue their wills to certain absolutes, such as family prayers, Sabbath observance, and rigorous study.

She suffered agonizing hurt when her brightest and most beautiful daughter became pregnant out of wedlock. But Susanna stood by her even though her austere husband, Samuel, never ceased his cruel reproaches.

She lived before women's rights and women's suffrage. She grew up in an Anglican pastor's home. She married an Anglican minister. He spent much of his time in debtors' prison because he simply did not know how to handle money. Consequently, she not only mothered this large family but also took up pastoral duties of the local Anglican church.

She refused to compromise her ideals. As a result, Susanna Wesley's children turned out to be exceptional achievers.

Perhaps you've heard of one son, Charles Wesley, the great hymn writer, and most certainly you know of John Wesley, the great preacher-reformer.

Did Susanna Wesley influence the world? Through her son John, she contributed to these tremendous accomplishments:

- the abolition of the slave trade
- the launching of the industrial revolution
- the establishment of the YMCA and YWCA
- the birth of the free hospital movement
- the multiplication of public libraries
- the creation of the Salvation Army

- the origination of the Barnardo homes (prototypes of today's orphanage movement)

- the founding of Methodism and the genesis of such great schools as the Wesleyan colleges, Asbury College, Albion College, Emory University, Southern Methodist University, and scores of other schools on both sides of the Atlantic

If you believe these developments changed the world, then you, too, must concede that Susanna Wesley goes down as one of history's most influential mothers. She must rank as one of the most successful people of all time.

She obeyed the Great Commission. She made it a priority. She was a time-management genius. She had to raise food and make bread, soups, and other modest but nutritious dishes. She had no car or even a horse and carriage. She walked wherever she went. She set aside one hour each week to pray for each of her children.

Time to Decide

Susanna Wesley didn't need the applause of her own generation in order to feel successful. Her eyes were on the future. She had little in the way of material advantages. Everything she gave to her children, she gave through the force of her character and personality. Yet what a legacy she left.

Think how many people achieve conventional success—money, position, respect, publicity—and then fritter away the precious opportunity to influence the world for good and for God.

The world says, "Achieve and enjoy. Celebrate your achievements—you've worked hard, and you deserve the rewards."

The Bible says, "Achieve and build. Enjoying your achievements is fine, but don't stop when you reach first base."

The world or the Bible—which are you going to listen to?

CHAPTER 7

The World Says "Just Do It"

The Bible Says "Before Everything, Pray"

AFTER ADDRESSING THE FACULTY and students of a leading Chinese university, I was asked who I considered to be the greatest leader of all time.

Without hesitation, I said, "Jesus." Surprisingly, all agreed. They then wanted me to tell them more about Jesus. Why was He so far ahead of the rest?

I cannot reproduce here everything I said, but prominent on the list was the fact that Jesus took prayer seriously. Start each day as Jesus did, and you will find a powerful building block for your successful life. "In the morning, having risen a long while before daylight, He went out and departed to a solitary place; and there He prayed" (Mark 1:35).

We see Him praying when He was popular and praying when He was unpopular. He was praying when He was baptized and when He was transfigured. After His busiest day's work, He retired to a solitary place and spent the whole night in prayer.

At other times, He rose a great while before day and went out into the mountains and prayed. He prayed at night after teaching all day in the temple and in the morning before entering into His busy day's work. He prayed before feeding the 5000 and again when the fragments were gathered up.

He prayed when taking the children up in His arms to bless them, and He prayed when one of His preachers came to Him and said, "Everyone is looking for You" (Mark 1:37).

He prayed in the Upper Room with His heartbroken disciples. He prayed in Gethsemane when under the very shadow of the cross. And He prayed at Calvary just before dropping His head on a pulseless chest and shouting, "It is finished."

No wonder His disciples said, "Lord, teach us to pray." Prayer is the hand that grasps the omnipotent hand. Don't expect personal success without prevailing prayer.

The Payoff Is Incalculable

When I was a student, I read that John Wesley awakened every morning at four and spent two hours in prayer. I determined to do the same. Every morning the alarm awakened me at four. I got on my knees by my bed—and quickly fell asleep.

The guilt I felt cancelled out any benefit of my good intentions. My frustration knew no bounds. Then I learned Wesley's secret. He went to bed at eight each night! So I decided to go to bed earlier and give myself eight hours of restorative sleep. Then I was able to arise before daybreak and spend time in prayer, Bible study, and meditation.

Solomon said in Ecclesiastes 1:16, "I communed with my heart, saying, 'Look, I have attained greatness, and have gained more wisdom than all who were before me in Jerusalem. My heart has understood great wisdom and knowledge.'" In other words, he spent quiet time with God.

The psalmist wrote, "My heart was hot within me; while I was musing, the fire burned. Then I spoke with my tongue" (Psalm 39:3). He probably wasn't "musing"—thinking and meditating—in the middle of a huge crowd at a noisy city intersection.

A quiet, solitary place will permit you to focus on your devotions. I refer to it as a place where you can hear yourself think.

Dr. William Lyon Phelps wrote, "I thoroughly believe in a university education for both men and women, but I believe knowledge of the Bible without a college education is more valuable than a college education without the Bible."[1]

Phelps spent many years as a professor at Yale University. He taught the first American university course on the modern novel. He was a brilliant speaker who drew huge crowds. He had a radio show in the early days of radio, wrote a syndicated newspaper column, lectured frequently, and published numerous popular books and articles. One could hardly accuse Phelps of being lopsided or a religious nut. He also wrote this:

> If you develop the absolute sense of certainty that powerful beliefs provide, then you can get yourself to accomplish virtually anything, including those things that other people are certain are impossible.

Doesn't that sound like the path to success? Phelps also made this note:

> The happiest people are those who think the most interesting thoughts. Those who decide to use leisure as a means of mental development, who love good music, good books, good pictures, good plays at the theater, good company, good conversation—what are they? They are the happiest people in the world; and they are not only happy themselves, they are the cause of happiness in others.

Set the Tone for Your Day

A psychiatrist in Atlanta once remarked to my brother Tom that whatever we think about in the first two minutes after awaking will determine our emotional state for the rest of the day. That made such an impression on Tom that ever since that time he has spent the first minutes of every day writing down four things for which he is grateful.

It's almost impossible to simultaneously be grateful and to worry, to be grateful and to hate, to be grateful and to criticize… to be grateful and to entertain any negative thought or utter any negative statements.

When I was a teenager, my father preached a sermon titled, "The Worst Sin." This was his text: "Although they knew God, they did not glorify Him as God, nor were thankful, but became futile in their thoughts, and their foolish hearts were darkened" (Romans 1:21).

He made the point that the worst sin is not unbelief, suicide, criticism…it is ingratitude. Ingratitude underlies all the rest.

Add to your emotional preparation a practical choice of place and time.

You may not have a place outside of your residence to which you can go, but you can surely find a place of privacy in your home. And you can surely rise before daybreak. This gives you an uninterrupted time before everything else in the house is stirring and you're distracted by the traffic in the streets.

Wesley got it right. You create time in the morning simply by going to bed at a decent hour and getting at least eight hours of uninterrupted sleep.

Psychologist David Seabury said that you need rest for the body but sleep for the mind. He opined that the freer you can be of psychic tension, the less sleep you need. Nevertheless, you do need rest for the body.

Before you go to sleep, take time to plan in detail your activities for the next day. Include meetings, personal visits, recreational activities—everything. Put a time factor beside each item to indicate precisely how much of the day you'll be assigning to each. One of the most productive leaders I have ever met—Paul J. Meyer—followed exactly this procedure.

The Midnight Visitor

In 1958, I was about to fall to sleep in a Tennessee motel when a thundering knock on my door disturbed me. It was my music director, who ignored my orders to go away. He would not stop knocking though I shouted at him to scram.

Finally he yelled through the door, "Haggai, how would you like to know about a friend of mine who can return to his room at two a.m. after an 18-hour day but refuse to go to sleep until he has planned in detail his next day?"

I said, "You've got my attention. Just a minute—I'll let you in."

He told me about Paul J. Meyer.

At that time Paul was 30 years old. He was born in a tent in California's Santa Clara Valley. He went to work at age eight. Before he was 25 he built the largest insurance agency in North America, recruiting 820 agents in 12 months at a time when the average agency had only 5 to 20 agents.

By 1955, Paul had become a millionaire at age 27—that amounts to $8,140,000 today. He was the youngest man ever to earn a seat at the Million Dollar Round Table in the insurance industry. He planned his schedule three years in advance, and he planned his giving five years in advance.

After recruiting 862 insurance salesmen, one Monday morning he walked into the offices to find them empty except for the carpet on the floor. The principals had absconded with the money and moved to another state.

Paul spent his entire fortune finding a solid position in another company for each salesman he had recruited. As he walked down the courthouse steps with Senator Claude Pepper, the Senator asked him how he felt.

"I'm broke," Paul responded.

Pepper replied, "Paul, you could have walked away from this mess and kept your personal fortune intact. You may not have any money left, but you have something of far greater worth. You have integrity. You are the wealthiest young man I know anywhere in the world."

Paul was not broke; he was just out of money. He was never poor. Poverty is a state of mind.

I submit to you that Paul would have not handled well the pressures to which he was subjected had it not been for the way he started every day—with prayer.

So step one is to plan the next day before you go to sleep at night. Visualize those plans as being fulfilled successfully and joyously. You will sleep better, and you will awaken in a positive mood instead of a negative mood.

The strength and direction Paul gained from his quiet time and the counsel of his pastor, Dr. William M. "Bill" Hinson, led him to talk to Jarrell McCracken, founder of a fledgling company called Word Records.

They had only two records out. One was of the Christmas story. Paul sold all the records that the company had in stock, and he sold them primarily to the Jewish people of the Miami Beach area. He reminded them that many of their Christian friends would be meeting with them over the holidays and that they ought to have some connection or bridge that would enhance the visits they had with their Christian friends.

It was brilliant.

Later, and again as a result of the Lord's direction during his quiet time, Paul made an agreement with McCracken that he would set up the entire marketing and sales network for Word Records. McCracken would pay all his expenses, but Paul would work strictly on a commission basis.

The first full year, Word made a net profit greater than they had ever imagined—$240,000. Paul's commissions amounted to $262,000! Word eventually became a prime American publishing company.

Dr. Hinson said to Paul, "You are happiest when you're showing people how to move to the outer limit of their potential. Why don't you get involved in something that will take advantage of your passion and your skill?"

That resulted in the formation of Success Motivation International.

By the time Paul passed away in 2009, he had sold more than $2.5 billion worth of materials. They had been translated into 24 languages in more than 60 countries. Just a single program, *The Dynamics of Personal Motivation*, racked up more than $700 million in sales.

The personal development courses he authored, if turned into books, would number more than 100 different volumes.

In addition to the training programs, he also wrote 21 books. And he wrote all of them between the ages of 70 and 81.

Paul J. Meyer's Secret

Although Paul was probably the best goal setter I have ever met, I don't think that was the secret of his success. It was his commitment to prayer.

I have a copy of his prayer journal. It's a five-by-eight three-ring leather notebook with his prayer points divided by categories. He clearly took his early morning quiet time seriously. He attributed the time he spent every morning with the Lord in prayer as the source of his motivation and his accomplishments.

He began every day with prayer and Bible study. When he saw my interest in that priority, he fashioned for me an eight-by-ten, seven-ring leather binder—a copy of his own devotional notebook. Everything he wrote is accompanied with relevant Scripture. He called it his Personal Prayer Journal. These are some of the ideas it includes:

- setting goals for the day
- finding a quiet place that is conducive for prayer

- sharing prayer goals with family members or a prayer partner
- avoiding distractions and interruptions
- updating the prayer journal at each prayer session
- prayer power—with nine supporting Bible passages
- personal prayer for growth
- prayers of praise
- a list of people prayed for (family, friends, social acquaintances)
- a list of ministries prayed for (church, charities, pastor, church leadership)
- special situations, current and ongoing
- specific health problems among family and friends
- a philosophy for living (including positive attitude, not worrying, gaining peace and contentment, and stewardship)

Every day Paul wrote his goals for the day on a set of three-by-five cards, which he kept inside his pocket calendar. In a special binder he filed his life goal, his long-term goals, and his near-term goals.

How did Paul amass his enormous fortune? How do we account for his positive influence in more than 190 nations? God empowered him and gave him favor. Paul personified the truth of Matthew 6:33: "Seek first the kingdom of God and His righteousness, and all these things shall be added to you."

Organized Prayer

"Prayer is not overcoming God's reluctance, but laying hold of God's willingness."[2] Lord Alfred Tennyson wrote these powerful words: "More things are wrought by prayer than this world dreams of."

I personally keep long lists of prayer items. These items include people, events, personal issues, financial actions, time management…I bring before the Lord anything and everything that concerns me.

The apostle Paul tells the Philippians to turn every care into a prayer. "Be anxious for nothing, but in everything by prayer and supplication, with thanksgiving, let your requests be made known to God" (Philippians 4:6). Notice that Paul says "everything." If it's big enough to concern you, it's big enough to pray about.

Further, I often put a date to the left of the item I'm praying about. When the answer comes, I put the date of the answer on the right-hand side.

Of course, certain things don't have any ending time. By nature, I am impatient. I pray for patience. I will probably be praying for patience as long as life shall last.

George Mueller, the great man of faith who built orphanages without any money in hand, prayed for the salvation of a friend for 52 years! The man did finally come to Christ!

Take your cares to the Lord. He can handle them. Your neighbor cannot—your neighbor has his or her own cares to worry about.

Let your calm demeanor be known to men and your prayers known to God.

The time you spend in prayer will multiply itself in positive productivity many times over.

The Bible Isn't Just a Book

In 1972, the late Paul Harvey, one of the globe's premiere radio and television newscasters, wrote me a letter to say he had started the habit of reading a chapter of the Bible every morning. He said he was amazed to see how that toned up the entire day. It enhanced his thoughts and actions until bedtime.

Paul Harvey was at his office in downtown Chicago before five every morning. He awakened at four, but he stopped long enough to start the day with a quiet time. This time turbocharged his day. It will do the same for you.

I have a friend who reads five Psalms and one chapter of Proverbs every morning. That takes him through the Psalms, which talk about our relationship with God, and the Proverbs, which talk about our relationship with others, once every month. He attributes his success to the wisdom and motivation he has derived from his Bible reading.

Reading the Bible systematically and daily will help you in many ways.

- It will improve your communications capability.

- It will enhance your attitude and give you wisdom for resolving difficulties that seem to defy solution.

- It will enlarge your vocabulary.

- It will give you insights into your daily living and into every aspect of your vocation.

- It will give you strength to overcome temptation that could unravel your reputation and your vocation.

In a recent sermon, Dr. David Allen of Fort Worth, Texas, referred to Romans 6 as "the Christian's obituary." He told about an executive who came to him weeping and said, "I have just been fired for viewing pornography on the Internet. How can I ever tell my wife the reason for my termination?"

How sad! Suppose he had spent that time reading the Bible instead of looking at pornography on the Web?

Don't Have Time for a Quiet Time?

You may say you don't have time for a quiet time at the beginning of the day.

My response is, "You don't have time *not* to have it." You will save so much time by starting the day with the proper mindset—which includes confidence, optimism, and faith—that you will achieve a great deal more than if you hit the ground running the minute you get out of bed.

I have benefited from not watching the newscast just before going to bed. Usually what constitutes news is just negative chatter. Positive stories rarely make the news. Instead, I find it highly profitable to engage in 15 to 30 minutes of light reading or listening to some uplifting music or other helpful recorded material. Then, after having planned the next day, I switch off the light. As I fall off to sleep, I visualize a continuum of successes beginning with the moment my eyes open in the morning.

Time to Decide

Marcus Aurelius said, "A man's life is what his thoughts make of it." But the Bible has an even better line: "As [a man] thinks in his heart, so is he" (Proverbs 23:7).

From the moment you awake, it is vital to discard thoughts, ideas, and worries that would curdle your day. If you allow these to take the ascendancy, you'll find yourself tired before your feet hit the ground. Soon you're running here and there, going through your morning hours unaware of your productivity-destroying activity.

The world says, "Just do it. After all, life is so full you can't really afford the time for activities as purposeless as reading your Bible and praying."

The Bible is far more realistic. Get yourself in sync with God at the beginning of the day and throughout the day, and everything else will tend to fall into place. Apart from anything else, the discipline you exercise prioritizing your quiet time will produce benefits in other areas. So the Bible says, "Before everything, pray."

The world or the Bible—which are you going to listen to?

CHAPTER 8

The World Says "Always Read the Fine Print"
The Bible Says "Keep It Simple"

YEARS AGO, AN 18-WHEELER TRUCK got stuck under an overpass. It couldn't go forward or backward.

Engineers were called to the scene and tried to come up with a solution as quickly as possible. But after hours of frustrating effort, they came up with nothing. Nada. Zilch.

Then a ten-year-old girl came on the scene and innocently asked, "Why don't you let some air out of the tires?" They did, reducing the height of the truck until it could move forward and release the traffic that had backed up for miles.

Too Much Information?

In 2007, researchers calculated the world's digital storage capacity at 295 exabytes. That's 295 with 20 zeros after it. And the number is going up every day.[1] Most of the information is probably useless. But even the tiny percentage that's real, solid, helpful learning, such as the contents of an encyclopedia, is far more than any single person could absorb and use.

You may be tempted to spread your net wide and try to master large and complex pieces of information, but the most useful and valuable things often turn out to be elegantly simple.

Recording that $E = mc^2$ requires very little of the world's digital memory. And although the details of the theory of relativity are beyond most of us, we can all understand the problem that prompted Einstein to think of it.

If two objects, he said, are traveling opposite directions at 50 miles per hour, then relative to each other, they are moving apart at 100 miles per hour. But if two objects are traveling in opposite directions at the speed of light, their combined speed cannot be twice the speed of light because nothing can travel faster than the speed of light.

Simplicity has many advantages in business. For example, the jet engine is far more efficient and powerful (and often quieter) than the piston engine. Its structure is also far simpler.

Truth Is Simple

In the Middle Ages, theologians spent many hours debating from Scripture just how many angels could balance on the point of a needle. Their obsession with complexity blinded them to the most important things. Divine truth doesn't require a PhD.

Concerning eternal salvation, the Bible says, "Whoever calls on the name of the LORD shall be saved" (Romans 10:13). Plenty of advertising taglines require more time to interpret than that!

Read the Ten Commandments in Exodus 20:2-17. Is any one of them difficult to understand?

> You shall have no other gods before Me.
>
> You shall not make for yourself a carved image—any likeness of anything that is in heaven above, or that is in the earth beneath, or that is in the water under the earth; you shall not bow down to them nor serve them. For I, the LORD your God, am a jealous God, visiting the iniquity of the fathers upon the children to the third and fourth generations

of those who hate Me, but showing mercy to thousands, to those who love Me and keep My commandments.

You shall not take the name of the LORD your God in vain, for the LORD will not hold him guiltless who takes His name in vain.

Remember the Sabbath day, to keep it holy. Six days you shall labor and do all your work, but the seventh day is the Sabbath of the LORD your God. In it you shall do no work: you, nor your son, nor your daughter, nor your male servant, nor your female servant, nor your cattle, nor your stranger who is within your gates. For in six days the LORD made the heavens and the earth, the sea, and all that is in them, and rested the seventh day. Therefore the LORD blessed the Sabbath day and hallowed it.

Honor your father and your mother, that your days may be long upon the land which the Lord your God is giving you.

You shall not murder.

You shall not commit adultery.

You shall not steal.

You shall not bear false witness against your neighbor.

You shall not covet your neighbor's house; you shall not covet your neighbor's wife, nor his male servant, nor his female servant, nor his ox, nor his donkey, nor anything that is your neighbor's.

Read Jesus' Beatitudes in Matthew 5:3-12:

Blessed are the poor in spirit,
    For theirs is the kingdom of heaven.
Blessed are those who mourn,

For they shall be comforted.
Blessed are the meek,
For they shall inherit the earth.
Blessed are those who hunger and thirst for
righteousness, For they shall be filled.
Blessed are the merciful,
For they shall obtain mercy.
Blessed are the pure in heart,
For they shall see God.
Blessed are the peacemakers,
For they shall be called sons of God.
Blessed are those who are persecuted for righteousness'
sake, For theirs is the kingdom of heaven.
Blessed are you when they revile and persecute you,
and say all kinds of evil against you falsely for My
sake. Rejoice and be exceedingly glad, for great is
your reward in heaven.

Are they not simple and easily understandable?

Jesus said, "You shall know the truth, and the truth shall make you free" (John 8:32). I cannot think of any truth He enunciated that is difficult to understand.

Education has much value and many rewards. But it doesn't always guide you to the truth or help you live a better or more successful life.

Bill Gates was a Harvard dropout. Steve Jobs was a Stanford dropout. Paul J. Meyer of Success Motivation International, mentioned earlier, was a college dropout. One of the most successful business tycoons in American history, Richard M. DeVos, never earned a bachelor degree. Thomas Edison did not have a grade school education. Henry Ford did not have a college education. Nor did Harvey Samuel Firestone.

All of these men were clever. But none of them made cleverness or complexity an end in itself. Their simplicity did not mean ease of achievement. It meant understanding what had to be done in order to achieve.

The Boss Who Raised Wages for His Own Good

Check out the great industrialists, and you'll find that those who succeeded stuck with the simplicity of their vision.

In January 1914, Henry Ford startled the world by announcing that Ford Motor Company would pay $5 a day to its workers. The average daily wage in the auto industry at that time was $2.34. Ford also reduced the workday from nine to eight hours. This rate didn't automatically apply to every worker, but it more than doubled the average autoworker's wage. This move started a small revolution in the automotive industry.

In 1913, to help meet the growing demand for the Model T, Henry Ford turned his attention to improving the manufacturing processes. The business model Ford developed—production on a grand scale performed by well-paid workers—proved very influential. It became the manufacturing standard for everything from vacuum cleaners to rockets.

Henry Ford saw that paying his workers well was good sense. He wanted to reduce worker attrition—labor turnover from monotonous assembly-line work was high—and he did it by fundamentally changing his relationship to the workforce. It was a synergy of business acumen and goodwill.

After Ford's announcement, thousands of prospective workers showed up at the Ford Motor Company employment office. People surged toward Detroit from the American South and even the nations of Europe.

As expected, employee turnover diminished. And by creating an eight-hour day, Ford could run three shifts instead of two, increasing productivity.

Ford reasoned that by building inexpensive cars in volume and raising wages, he could sell more cars to employees. The $5, eight-hour day helped better the lot of all American workers and contributed to the emergence of the American middle class. In the process, Henry Ford had changed manufacturing forever.

It was a simple idea that bore massive results.

Few Words Chosen Carefully

Ted Nicholas, whose copy writing and publishing has resulted in more than $7 billion in sales, said, "The basic truths about marketing are the same now, and will be the same 50 years from now, a 100 years from now, 1000 years from now." He then goes on to say that one of the great things about marketing is that "things are changing so rapidly; it's great to know some things will never change."

According to Nicholas, "73 percent of the buying decision is made at the point of the headline."[2] Other communication experts agree. They further agree that the headline should not be more than 17 words.

Any way you read that, it spells simplicity.

On average, eight out of ten people will read headline copy, but only two out of ten will read the rest! This is the secret to the power of the headline.

Nicholas takes two weeks to write a letter. He spends 12 of the 14 days in writing headlines. He may fill 200 or 300 three-by-five cards with one possible headline on each card. He then decides which will be the best.

Hard work? Absolutely. Simple to understand what must be done? Yes.

One of the best books on communication to come across my desk in the past 25 years is *How to Get Your Point Across in 30 Seconds or Less* by Milo O. Frank. Thirty seconds will equal about 60 words.

In his book, Frank shows that if you can't put your point across in 30 seconds, you probably can't put it across at all. Simplicity is the key.

The world's top copywriters agree that one of the greatest ways to open a headline is with the simple words, "How to." Everybody finds those words intriguing.

I am told that Amazon carries 7000 books with "how to" in the title.

A cherished friend of mine received a nasty, libelous letter and wrote one of the best replies I've ever read. His brilliantly simple response increased my appreciation of him. My friend founded and chaired the largest American public relations and advertising company dealing with nonprofit organizations.

The sender was respected in some circles, but his letter was foul, false, and fatuous. Just reading it raised my blood pressure, and it wasn't even addressed to me. My friend looked at it, read it, shrugged his shoulders, and laughed.

He could have engaged a battery of lawyers and sued the author of the letter for libel. But he was too busy for such foolishness. And it violated his style of simplicity. He simply wrote this on the bottom of the letter: "Charlie [not his real name], some idiot wrote me this letter and had the audacity to sign your name. I thought you ought to know about it. Sam."

I nearly went into hysterics. It was a classic response. Case closed. How do you answer a letter like that? "Charlie" never bothered him again.

Nothing Is Too Hard for Simplicity

Once again let me remind you that simplicity does not mean ease of execution. Writing a 17-word headline takes 12 days for the world's highest-paid copywriter. What makes you think you can do it in less time?

However, when you follow the simple rules and write or speak in a way that (1) gets the listener's attention, (2) keeps his interest, (3) possibly tells a wonderful story that makes your case, and (4) presents your request—all in 30 seconds, you have arrived! You'll save time and accomplish more than you ever thought possible. And you'll find that it's fun.

According to legend, Mark Twain was asked how long he would need to prepare a speech. He said, "If you want a 20-minute speech, it will take two weeks. If you want a 30-minute speech, it will take one week. If you want an hour speech, I can come tomorrow."

When it comes to communicators, only speakers who thoroughly know their subjects can deliver them in clear and simple language.

The same is true with parenthood. Long years ago I concluded that the most successful parents are those who have few rules—but rules that cannot be broken or bent. Where rules are easy to remember and fairly enforced, you usually find the most stable and happiest children.

After all, God limited the Commandments to ten.

Time to Decide

In the Bible, complexity marks the character of Satan, whereas simplicity marks the character of God. Consider for instance the phrase "the fruit of the Spirit." It is singular and simple. The Scripture follows it with the various facets of that truth—love, joy, peace, and so on.

On the other hand, when Jesus asked a demoniac, "What is your name?" the satanic network in control of the man cried out, "My name is Legion, for we are many."

"The fruit of the Spirit *is*…" (singular). In the same passage in Galatians 5, we read, "The works of the flesh *are*…" (plural).

The world says, "Always read the small print—the more you know, the more fronts on which you attack the problem, the greater your advantage."

The Bible underlines the truth of what we have all experienced when it says, "Keep it simple."

The world or the Bible—which are you going to listen to?

CHAPTER 9

The World Says "Aim to Win"

The Bible Says "Put Character Before Career"

When I attended Stony Brook School for Boys in 1937, the three-word motto of the school impressed itself on my mind, and I admire it to this day: Character Before Career.

Did Stony Brook's appeal derive only from its highly cerebral faculty? From its prestigious history? From its high teacher-to-student ratio? From its idyllic location and campus? From its superb athletic program? Other institutions offer these things, but Stony Brook embraced a value system that set it apart from other schools.

Education that does not issue from character rooted in the gospel creates mischief that eats at the vitals of society. Education alone will not make up for lack of character.

When I was young man, I read an article that referred to the high number of PhDs incarcerated in Sing Sing Correctional Facility.

Fifty-seven percent of Hitler's SS troops had master's degrees. And in the 1930s, Germany was considered the most erudite nation in the Western world. For example, Heidelberg University was a favorite for post-doctoral studies in the early twentieth century. Seven of the ten people involved in the Manhattan Project, which led to the atomic bomb, were Germans.

The behavior of both Hitler's SS troops and Sing Sing's intellectual inmates proved that their moral brakes were not sufficient for their mental horsepower. The proliferation of courses on ethics in our universities spells out the universal awareness that character has been under attack.

Consider for example the matter of truthfulness. The Bible says, "Let your 'Yes' be 'Yes' and your 'No,' 'No'" (James 5:12). But now we not only disregard that injunction but also violate the ninth commandment: "You shall not bear false witness against your neighbor." Today we euphemize falsehood with the word "spin." Communication has given way to *mis*communication, and order has given way to dissimulation.

Consider also the matter of personal safety. I was 14 years old in 1938 when I returned to Stony Brook after Christmas holiday. I traveled from Boston to New York City by bus. With my flimsy suitcase in one hand and my tattered briefcase in the other, I found my way to the subway station and boarded the subway to Jamaica, a neighborhood in Queens. From Jamaica, I took a train to Stony Brook on the north shore of Long Island.

Prior to Mayor Giuliani's cleaning up New York City, can you imagine a 14-year-old making that trip alone in the blackness of night?

By character, I mean moral strength. By moral, I refer to the goodness or badness of behavior, the distinction of right and wrong, the relationship to accepted rules and standards of Christ-honoring behavior.

Make Yourself a Motto

Tony Robbins, the world's most highly paid motivational speaker (he recently made more than $130 million in one year), recognizes the power of words. He calls his affirmations "incantations." The magazine *ASAP*, put out by Forbes, provides this quote from Robbins:

> When you incant what you want over and over again,
>   you begin to focus on it…The statement I "incant"

aloud while I'm running or driving—so that my body is in a peak state—is my mission statement: The purpose of my life is to humbly serve our Lord by being a loving, playful, powerful, and passionate example of the absolute joy that is available to us the moment we rejoice in God's gifts and sincerely love and serve all of His creations.

"Incantation" is another word for a motto.

Mottoes are designed to stick in the mind. Advertisers talk about "single-minded propositions." Once an ad agency has determined what a client company wants to achieve, it reduces this aspiration to a single-minded proposition—the single, essential message that the client company wants to put across. Mottoes fulfill the same function. They express the very core of an institution's message.

But there's a difference between a motto and an advertising jingle, such as "Coke Is It" or the Lexus ad "The Relentless Pursuit of Perfection." Mottoes aren't superficial. They are rooted deep down in common values and essential beliefs.

I cannot think of a better way to develop strong character, underlying a successful career, than to daily reflect on this motto: Character Before Career. Why not place these words in your bedroom, your office, your wallet, the windshield visor of your car? Imagine how much you would benefit from repeating these words several times daily.

Suppose you, your family members, and your staff were to repeat daily (or oftener) with passion, "By God's grace, I purpose this day to think, speak, and act in accordance with my values, which are consonant with the Word of God and which put character before career." Can you imagine the resulting success in every area of life?

In the Scripture, James writes in chapter three about the power of the tongue. The more we focus on God-honoring values and repeat those values, the more our speech will impact our lives. If our self-talk focuses on success, our successes will lead us to greater heights.

The more you focus your self-talk on the goals consistent with successful values, the more integrated and successful your life will be. A continuing habit of repeating, acting on, and vitalizing this motto will empower you daily toward success.

Mark Victor Hansen's *Chicken Soup for the Soul* series was rejected by publishers more than 100 times but eventually sold 55 million copies. Hansen says, "What you visualize, you energize."

Only when you internalize your motto will it influence your behavior.

Andrew Carnegie understood the power of internalized concepts. If you visit his Skibo Castle in Scotland, you will see the sayings that he considered important beautifully mounted on the walls.

The Israelites internalized and repeated the affirmation, "The Lord our God is one God."

Your motto must be more than a statement; it must become a life-controlling ritual.

A Remarkable School

I went to school from a godly home. My father and mother walked the talk. When Dad died in his 92nd year, he had read the Bible through 103 times. He was a linguist, conversant in seven languages. When Dad was away from home, Mother led our mandatory family devotions.

My parents sent me to Stony Brook to provide me with a superior education, not to improve my environment.

I must tell you that in more than 100 trips around the world and more than a score of intercontinental trips, I have reflected hundreds of times on the tremendous contributions Stony Brook made to me both in and out of the classroom.

At Stony Brook I met and mixed with other nationalities. My time there had the effect of putting me at ease with people of all backgrounds. My closest friend was a Brazilian, Percival Gomm. My roommate was the son of missionary parents, the Nicholsons.

There I developed an appreciation for ritual and protocol. Chapel services. Coat and tie at meals. Special events involving great music and great speaking.

At one chapel service, the venerable world statesman Dr. John R. Mott spoke. He changed and elevated my concept of world evangelism. I shall never forget this man, in his seventies, speaking to us about the challenge of world missions. I was 13 at the time.

Mott single-handedly raised more than $300 million (over $6 billion in today's US dollars) from 1895 to 1933 for Christ-centered causes worldwide. He wrote more than 40 books. He recruited 246,000 people from America to Australia into Christian vocation. The mind-stretching challenge of Dr. John R. Mott impacted my life and had a great deal to do with the organization I founded 43 years ago.

Another example of the motto Character Before Career was Dr. Frank E. Gaebelein, the founder of Stony Brook. He ranks as a success by every criterion I know, and he personified the motto. I could never be the same after hearing this man.

The tensile strength and gentle character of the scholarly Dr. Gaebelein made an impression upon me that lasts to this day. His personal interest in each student serves as a model to school leaders. I still have letters he wrote to my parents about me. What a treasure!

He lived out daily the truth of the motto. He was not only an educator but also a world-class classical pianist and globally influential author. He also personified success and the impact of this motto in his personal life, leadership, and global influence.

The Washerwoman Who Taught the Professors

Bringing our behavior into sync with our value system leads to integration of character. And only the person with this integration of character can be said to have integrity. Without integrity, character is flawed and success is undermined.

I find it strange that even as universities are speeding to outdo each other in their development of ethics departments, current ethical levels are spiraling downward. The trend in high schools is no less problematic. Here are some recent findings from the Josephson Institute.

> The 2010 Report Card included some 40,000 students across the nation. Results showed that most young people feel that ethics and character are important on both a personal level and in business, but they express very cynical attitudes about whether a person can be ethical and succeed. Moreover, an alarming number of students admitted to recently lying, cheating, and stealing.[1]

Good character emerges with or without the help of university departments that study ethics.

Mrs. Oseola McCarty worked as a washerwoman, having been forced to drop out of school in the sixth grade to care for her family. She astounded the nation with her gift of $150,000 to set up a scholarship for needy students, money she saved from eight decades of labor. Her story teaches everyone the true meaning of generosity, grace, and humility. That's character-producing success.

Character Is Shaped Early

Unfortunately, success alone doesn't produce character. And without the foundation of character, success satisfies only as long as it continues. Take it away, and there's little to fall back on. At 36 years of age, Lord Byron wrote these words:

> My days are in the yellow leaf;
> The flowers and fruits of love are gone;
> The worm, the canker, and the grief
> Are mine alone!

One of the most heartrending articles I ever read appeared on page 1 of the *New York Times* on May 21, 1931. It detailed the suicide of Ralph Barton.

Barton was an outstanding cartoonist—one of the nation's highest paid. And he was a great writer. In his suicide note, he described the melancholy he had been suffering. Apparently his fears nearly drove him mad. He included this in the note:

> It [melancholia] has prevented my getting anything like the full value out of my talent, and, for the past three years, has made work a torture to do at all. It has made it impossible for me to enjoy the simple pleasures of life that seem to get other people through. I have run from wife to wife, from house to house, and from country to country, in a ridiculous effort to escape from myself…
>
> No one is responsible for this—no one person except myself…
>
> I've done it because I'm fed up with inventing devices for getting through twenty-four hours every day and with bridging over a few months periodically with some purely artificial interest, such as a new "gal" who annoys me to the point where I forgot my own troubles.[2]

Did success bring this wealthy, highly paid writer-cartoonist the stability and satisfaction he sought? No—because at the level of character, he was running from himself and destroying his relationships. How tragic that a life such as his, pregnant with great possibilities for blessing his generation in the will of God, had to end in such tragedy!

Character should be the bottom line of human life. But we live in an age where the bottom line is always economics. The one ability we cannot do without is the ability to earn money, so we easily put career before character, not character before career.

But people who live by this pattern often lead desperately unhappy lives. (Gordon Gecko in the 1987 film *Wall Street* has many counterparts in the real world.) The greed that helps motivate them as financiers often goes along with weak-mindedness and corruptibility. Why? Personal appetite has usurped the top spot on their list of values. Anyone who feeds that sick appetite gets their attention.

Character Equals Strength

History tells us that the people most of us admire were unselfish and determined to stick by their principles. This is the essence of sainthood—and of good leadership. William Wallace, Winston Churchill, Abraham Lincoln, Nelson Mandela—they all share this characteristic.

I believe that this kind of unselfishness has its roots in the gospel. Those who make the effort to do good almost inevitably end up feeling that they are incapable of doing it—which is precisely where Christian discipleship begins.

In Romans 7:18-24 (NIV), the apostle Paul wrote, "I have the desire to do what is good, but I cannot carry it out. For I do not do the good I want to do, but the evil I do not want to do—this I keep on doing…What a wretched man I am! Who will rescue me from this body of death?"

But then he adds, "Thanks be to God, who delivers me through Jesus Christ our Lord…Therefore there is now no condemnation for those…who do not live according to the flesh but according to the Spirit" (7:25–8:4).

The Grecian says, "Man, know thyself."

The Roman says, "Man, rule thyself."

The Chinese says, "Man, improve thyself."

The Brahman says, "Man, submerge thyself in the universal sum of all."

The Muslim says, "Man, submit thyself."

But the Lord Jesus Christ says, "Without Me you can do nothing."

This is why we find Paul making the extraordinary claim in Philippians 4:13, "I can do all things through Christ who strengthens me." That's the key to the character that transforms life and ennobles career.

The Country That Almost Died

Eighteenth-century England provides one of history's great illustrations of the restoration of character bringing about radically positive changes in the nation.

What a mess Europe was during the early part of the eighteenth century! Agnostics were having a field day. The books of Morgan and Hume—and in the nineteenth century, Thomas Huxley—with their denials of all that was spiritually right and noble, were published and scattered with reckless abandon. The populace in general regarded Christianity as a pipe dream and ridiculed its teachings. Voltaire was the most popular writer across the continent. Frederick the Great was a practical atheist. Men everywhere were hailing the disappearance of Christianity.

In those days, believing in the inspiration of the Bible meant being denied membership in the literary circles of Germany. Rationalism spread like a prairie fire in Norway, and Scotland languished under a starless spiritual midnight. The ministry had deviated from its message, and preachers were referred to as "the apes of Epictetus."

Morality collapsed. Empty heads in the pulpits preached to empty spaces in the pews. Even some preachers reveled during the week in drinking and carousals.

Revolution was on in France. In the streets of London, gin shops offered to sell enough gin for a penny to make one drunk, or enough for twopence to give a dead drunk. Freethinking clubs were everywhere. Crimes and outrages were perpetrated in broad daylight in the streets of London. England was headed for a revolution.

The deterministic, fatalistic, and materialistic teachings of these agnostics saturated the thinking of the people and snapped the fetters of moral restraint.

Just a few young men of true character listened to God's call to save the country from impending doom. God raised up men like John and Charles Wesley and George Whitefield, who became flaming evangels and carried the Bible message across the nation. As they preached the Bible doctrines of sin, hell, grace, and salvation, people turned from sin. Multitudes of hearers, often in tears, clutched at these preachers' garments as they spoke.

George Whitefield preached 300 times from the text, "Ye must be born again." Asked why, he responded, "Because ye must be born again."

Multitudes wrestled with God in prayer during all-night prayer meetings. Great revivals swept the country. Bible societies became more prominent than literary societies. And in the wake of the revitalized evangelical preaching came a higher standard of living.

The impact of this evangelical preaching was to be felt all over the world.

- John Howard instituted prison reforms in Europe.

- J. Hudson Taylor founded the China Inland Mission in the next century, which by 1910 had sent out 968 missionaries.

- John Barnardo began his mission work in London, which resulted in the rescuing and training of 70,000 homeless children.

- William Booth organized the Salvation Army, which was to encircle the globe.

- Princeton University, the University of Pennsylvania, and many other universities are tributes to the evangelical preaching of George Whitefield.

God used the gospel in all its simplicity to produce character that saved a civilization and purified the stream of humanity.

God has a high calling for you too. I pray that you will achieve success with that vocation, whatever it may be. But remember that the road to success leads first to character. Character *before* career. That way you'll be remembered for something worthwhile.

Character Talks

In 1943 the Lord permitted Christine Barker to become a successful vocalist, but she wanted to use her talents for God's glory rather than personal acclaim. Thinking of attending Chicago's Moody Bible Institute, she thumbed through the current student annual. One of the photographs immediately fascinated her. It was of me.

When she attended a Monday morning convocation in the old Torrey-Gray auditorium, she saw the person in the photograph. Her heart sank.

First, she scarcely recognized me from the picture—compared to the other students I looked as if I'd come from the other side of the world. Which in a way I had. My father came from Syria, my mother from a British-American background. I have long had to admit, however, that the map on my face is not London; it's Damascus.

In her first observation, Chris sized me up as being from some off-brand Christian denomination, and being a stalwart Baptist herself, she knew she could never entertain another serious thought about me. She put me completely out of mind.

Chris says that one time, she and I were alone on the school elevator but that I paid her no attention. On another occasion I don't recall, she says we brushed shoulders on the street. It wasn't that I was impervious to a beautiful young lady. It was preoccupation, perhaps so-called absentmindedness.

A little later my cousin Marge, also a student at Moody, said to me, "John, I just met a darling girl from Bristol, Virginia—a real Southern belle."

I informed her that women were not to be a part of my life until I finished my education. I asserted my intention to eliminate all dating until my studies were completed.

One Saturday morning, waiting for the taxi to take me to the train station for a weekend preaching assignment, I saw Marge and this beautiful young woman coming down the steps of the Moody post office. Marge introduced us, and then they went into the snack shop. Casually but very much on purpose, I walked in front of that snack shop as often as I could until the taxi arrived.

We fell in love, and I proposed to Chris on our third date. My dad couldn't understand why anyone would propose on the third date. "It seemed as though the second date was a little too soon," I told him.

Chris's character impressed me as much as her looks. The tragic injury to our son Johnny effectively tied her to the house for two decades, and yet she remained a shining example and powerful witness.

For example, one day the power company sent a new man to read the meter at our house.

"Lovely day, isn't it?" Chris remarked, letting him in.

"Depends on how you look at it," he grumbled.

"Oh," my wife countered, "the Bible says, 'This is the day the LORD has made; we will rejoice and be glad in it.'"

The meter man stopped, looked at his order sheet, and snapped, "You're a preacher's wife. Got a free house and everything. They probably give your husband a car and pay for the gas. People like you don't know what it's like to have it tough."

Chris smiled and showed him where to find the meter.

When he came back he headed straight for the door, but Chris intercepted him. "Would you mind stepping into the other room a minute?" she asked. "I'd like you to meet our son."

The young man reluctantly followed.

There lay Johnny, sprawled out on his special bed, his big dark eyes wide with greeting, a smile broad upon his face.

"Johnny," Chris said, "this is our meter man. Young man, I would like you to meet Johnny."

That afternoon the meter man went to Georgetown, Kentucky. While there, visiting friends, he told them about the experience with Johnny and what an impact it had made on him.

The friends he was visiting lived next door to a couple who had a daughter with cerebral palsy. They were extremely bitter about their daughter's condition. After the meter man left, his friends told their neighbors the story of Chris's poise and charm and the unusual experience the meter man had meeting Johnny.

The parents of the cerebral palsied daughter were so impressed that they went to a local church that very night and were both converted. They became active members of the church.

Time to Decide

> He has shown you, O man, what is good;
> And what does the LORD require of you
> But to do justly,
> To love mercy,

And to walk humbly with your God?
(Micah 6:8).

The world says, "Aim to win—and let nothing stand in your way. The workplace is a competitive environment, and succeeding means winning." Career, then, gets stripped down to power, money, and looks.

The Bible points out that winning in itself has limited value and doesn't deliver lasting satisfaction. The Bible's emphasis isn't on building your résumé but on building your value as a person. To the extent that we have influence, we have a responsibility to guide others—family, children, friends, colleagues, casual acquaintances, and perhaps even fans—toward something worthwhile. The Bible says, "Put character before career."

The world or the Bible—which are you going to listen to?

CHAPTER 10

The World Says "Look Out for Number One"
The Bible Says "Give and Be Wealthy"

In the late 1930s, Fred and Grace Kinser listened every Sunday night to *The Old-Fashioned Revival Hour*, featuring Dr. Charles E. Fuller from Pasadena, California. At that time Fuller was one of America's premier nondenominational radio broadcasters.

The Kinsers didn't have much money. Fred was a bread salesman with a modest income, and Grace was a stay-at-home wife and mother. They sent small offerings (in reality, large offerings compared to their resources) and prayed fervently for the radio ministry. Eventually, Grace developed a burning passion to send more money. She knew Dr. Fuller needed money to maintain the broadcast and enlarge its outreach.

So Grace made salads and sandwiches and sold them from door to door. Her efforts grew into a major business. She became Dr. Fuller's largest donor before he died, and in the process she became a multimillionaire. Not long before her death she sold the entire business, Mrs. Kinser's Salads, for millions of dollars.

I met Grace Kinser. She told me with a chuckle, "John, many women in my neighborhood said, 'Well, Grace, with all due respect, we can make better salads than you.' But there was one difference. Unlike them, I actually went out and did it."

The Craziest Advice Ever

As I write, America, Europe, and many other parts of the world languish under the most severe economic downturn since the Great Depression. Millions of people across America struggle with mortgages that are significantly higher than the current value of their homes.

Many have had to downsize their expenditures in order to survive. Teenage children accustomed to driving their own automobiles have been forced to give them up. Because they were reared in an atmosphere in which net worth and self-worth were confused, they struggle with the emotional trauma.

Parents have had to take their children out of pricey private schools and put them into the public schools. This adds to the humiliation and the perceived diminishing of self-worth.

Many high school seniors whose minds had been set on the expensive Ivy League schools now cope with the reality that the money is not there. They are altering their plans and hoping to get into much cheaper state universities—which, by the way, may not be that far behind the Ivy League schools academically.

In times like these, prioritized giving may seem strange indeed. Surely you give after you've secured your own financial survival, right?

But remember the motto from the last chapter: Character Before Career.

You will do well to study the giving mindset of America's greatest tycoons. I refer to such men as William Colgate, J.L. Kraft, Robert G. LeTourneau, John Wanamaker, Robert Woodruff of Coca-Cola fame, S. Truett Cathy of Chick-fil-A, Mary Crowley of Home Interiors and Gifts, Mr. and Mrs. Leland Stanford of Stanford University...the list seems never to end.

In most of the instances, the superrich started with virtually no money at all. Some of them were broke on more than one occasion.

But they were never poor. Poverty, as I said earlier, is a state of mind. Here is God's promise:

> Give, and it will be given to you: good measure, pressed down, shaken together, and running over will be put into your bosom. For with the same measure that you use, it will be measured back to you (Luke 6:38).

Often Christians will say to me, "That promise relates only to Christians."

Rubbish.

If an atheist jumps off of a 30-story building, he will be dead. So will a Christian. The law of gravity has no favorites. And neither does the law of sowing and reaping. If an atheist plants a thousand acres of corn, he will enjoy a greater harvest than a Christian who plants only ten acres of corn.

Net Worth Does Not Indicate Self-Worth

I have met with multiplied thousands of leaders. In the halls of government, the campuses of universities, and the boardrooms of commerce, their conversations reveal that many of these people (even some believers) rate their self-worth in terms of their net worth.

If financial adversities prevent them from wearing expensive clothes, joining exclusive clubs, enrolling their children in prestigious schools, and living in multimillion-dollar homes in gated communities—in short, attaining a certain social cachet and luxurious standard of living—their self-worth takes a nosedive.

It's sad—and unnecessary.

In the very first chapter of the Bible, God emphasized the truth that He is the owner of all things. His name is mentioned 15 times in the first 14 verses, 31 times in the first chapter, and 45 times in the first two chapters! What point is God making? He is owner of all. He has not transferred the title deed to anyone.

Jesus spoke more about money than He did any other subject.

He mentions money 88 times in the Gospel of Matthew, 54 times in the Gospel of Mark, and 92 times in the Gospel of Luke.

Sixteen out of His 38 parables had to do with the right and wrong use of material possessions.

One out of every six verses of the four Gospels has to do with the right and wrong use of material possessions.

Don't you think that if Jesus spoke more about money than anything else, we would be wise to pay special attention?

You cannot win genuine and lasting success without the habit of financial generosity.

Once again reread Luke 6:38. You will do yourself a favor by memorizing it and repeating it every morning when you have your quiet time.

That exercise will liberate you from the self-destructive habits of whining, complaining, and blaming.

Giving should be habitual.

Ted Nicholas, who has produced more than $7 billion of revenue from his writing, is 77 years of age as I write these words. He has residences in Switzerland, Cyprus, and the United States. By his own testimony, he has more money than he could ever spend.

So why does he continue to work? So he can give more money to charities.

No wonder he has a positive mental attitude. I have never known a miser who was a positive thinker.

Givers enjoy robust mental health.

I heard psychologist Dr. Alfred Adler say that he had never known anybody who was neurotic while totally immersed in helping other people.

That goes for givers.

The Financier Who Bucked the Trend

I considered Sir John Templeton a dear and cherished friend. Three times he visited me in Atlanta, and three times he invited me to visit his home at Lyford Cay in the Bahamas.

He was at Yale University when the Great Depression struck. His father wrote and told him that because of the change in fortune, John would have to come home. The father could no longer afford the tuition.

John replied, "Will you let me stay here if I provide for my own financial needs?"

The father acquiesced. John Templeton made it all the way through Yale. With the help of hard work and scholarships, he graduated at the top of his class with a degree in economics. He then attended Oxford University for two years on a Rhodes Scholarship.

After completing his studies, the 24-year-old Templeton made a tour of 35 countries with James Inksetter—a fellow Christian from Oxford. They watched their pennies, and with creative thrift, they completed their trip on a very modest budget.

Templeton began his career on Wall Street with the firm Fenner and Beane. He held stocks for an average of four years and looked for bargains that were largely ignored. In 1939, he borrowed money to buy 100 shares of each penny stock selling at one dollar or less per share. His investment almost quadrupled in the space of four years.

He and his first wife (later killed in an accident) saved 50 percent of their income so he could open his own firm, which he did. He started the first international investment fund.

He believed in tithing—and he practiced it. He believed in prayer—and he practiced it. He said, "If you begin with prayer, you will think more clearly and make fewer mistakes." He was equally eloquent in his emphasis on the value of tithing.

You may have heard of the Templeton Prize for Progress in Religion, which honors a person who made the greatest contribution to religion during the year. For the past few years, the cash value of the attending honor amounted to more than $1 million.

Did Templeton's generosity harm him financially? He died a billionaire!

Pick the Right Metaphor

Most people consider everything they have as a large pie. They look at any gift they make as a piece of the pie that diminishes its size and the value.

That's not a helpful metaphor. Instead, consider everything you have as grains of wheat. The more you plant, the greater your harvest.

Obviously, most folks don't believe that. Fewer than 2.6 percent of church members tithe their money. I doubt that the percentage of unchurched people is higher! Clearly, most people do not understand the law of sowing and reaping.

The wisest man of all time, Solomon, said, "The generous soul will be made rich, and he who waters will also be watered himself" (Proverbs 11:25). Solomon was right, and he was not talking about heaven. He's talking about temporal as well as spiritual prosperity. You will never achieve true success without generosity.

The Reason Why It's Vital to Give

God doesn't need your gifts.

Do you think He reads the *Wall Street Journal,* the *Financial Times,* or *Investor's Business Daily?* Do you think He consults with financial gurus? Do you think His wealth fluctuates with the price of gold? He says,

> Every beast of the forest is Mine,
> And the cattle on a thousand hills…

> If I were hungry, I would not tell you;
> For the world is Mine, and all its fullness
> (Psalm 50:10,12).

You do not give because God needs your money. You give because you need to.

In the Garden of Eden, God set aside one tree that Adam and Eve were to leave alone. Why? He wanted to remind Adam and Eve that He is the owner of all things.

When you squander God's tithe, you are repeating in kind, if not in degree, the sin of Adam and Eve. Like them, you are taking that which God has reserved for Himself.

Again, God has never transferred the title deed to anyone. We are His stewards.

If I put some money in the hands of my broker, he profits in proportion to the degree that he is successful in enhancing that corpus. The steward's responsibility is to enhance what has been entrusted to him or to her. What an opportunity we have! What a joy it is!

Do you think you are wiser than God? Do I think for one moment that I can do better with my money if I keep it all than I can if I give God His tenth?

We also give in simple appreciation of divine grace. You cannot earn your salvation. The Bible says we are saved by grace, not by our own works. Grace is God giving to you and me all that He requires from us.

What does God require? Righteousness. Grace is God giving me that righteousness in Jesus Christ. He is my righteousness. I cannot buy it. And the grace I receive does not increase because of merit or decrease because of demerit.

The apostle Paul says in Romans 11:32, "God has committed them all to disobedience, that He might have mercy on all." And there is no such thing as mild sin. You may be a finely veneered example of sartorial perfection with no blemishes on your complexion, but in God's sight you're as bad a sinner as the hog-jawed, red-nosed son of perdition who rolls drunk in the gutter. God has "committed them all to disobedience."

So we can't pay for grace—but we can show appreciation for it. "By grace you have been saved through faith, and that not of yourselves; it is the gift of God, not of works, lest anyone should boast" (Ephesians 2:8-9).

Not Just Money

Again, don't focus only on the money when you give.

Paul writes in Romans 12:1, "I beseech you therefore, brethren, by the mercies of God, that you present your bodies…" He didn't say heart. He didn't say head or intellect. He said bodies—the bodies that we Christians have made into temples of the Holy Spirit.

> Do you not know that your body is the temple of the
> Holy Spirit, who is in you, whom you have from God,
> and you are not your own? For you were bought at a
> price; therefore glorify God in your body and in your
> spirit, which are God's (1 Corinthians 6:19-20).

Clearly I can't climb into the offering plate. So how do I present my body? The answer is in the dimensions that the body occupies: time and energy. If my earthly time is up, my body can do nothing. If I have no energy, my body cannot function.

So when I put money in the offering plate, I am not making a conscience payment to God. I am demonstrating my surrender of life and talent to Him.

One of the greatest gifts I have ever received on behalf of Haggai Institute was the encouragement of a major donor. Ed Prince was the progenitor of the Prince Corporation, which produced much of the inside material for most automobiles. He built the company from its original capitalization of $5,000 to a colossus that sold shortly after his death for more than $1 billion.

He and his wife, Elsa, attended a Haggai Institute training session for non-Western leaders. On the Saturday night of their visit, he arranged for me to have dinner with his family. This man of unspeakable vision, who had stunned the industrial world with his achievements, looked across the long table at me and said, "John, are you sure your vision is big enough for the next 50 years?"

I could have wept. I did weep inside—a weeping of gratitude. I reflected on those early days when even closest friends, wanting to be charitable, soft-pedaled their criticism. But they let me know they thought it was a wild scheme. Now this captain of industry endorsed the program. He wanted to be sure that my vision was large enough for the next half century.

Time to Decide

In 1950, I met one of Chicago's leading businessmen and philanthropists, Paul Brandel. We had a delightful conversation, and he told me his story.

He had graduated with a law degree just shortly before he went into the military during World War II in 1941. During his time in the service, he decided he did not want to practice law when he got out; he would much prefer business. For one thing, business would have fewer time constraints. Also, he would have greater freedom because he would be working for himself and not serving as the legal counsel for a host of other people.

So when he mustered out of the service, he took all the money he had saved and put together his first small business deal. He projected what he thought would be a good return on that investment. He didn't say, "Well, if the Lord blesses me, I'm going to give a tithe." Instead, he borrowed the money to give 30 percent of his *anticipated* profit. He borrowed it personally, and he gave the 30 percent of his anticipated profit to the Lord *before* he started the project.

He followed that principle until his death at age 74.

I don't want you to get the impression that every deal he made turned out to be a winner. Far from it. What farmer has never had a failed crop? Yet throughout his life, Brandel followed that principle of giving—30 percent of his anticipated profit before he executed any venture.

He made millions. He gave to hospitals and schools. He strongly supported foreign missions. He well understood "second mile" giving. He also understood that giving should be on the front end, just as you sow seed before you get the harvest and invest your time in study before you get the degree.

Paradoxically, because of God's generosity, that is the best way of looking after number one.

The world says, "Look after number one." In other words, give only the leftovers.

The Bible says, "Give and be wealthy."

The world or the Bible—which are you going to listen to?

CHAPTER 11

The World Says "Accept Who You Are"
The Bible Says "Train Your Mind"

ONE DAY MY WIFE received an anonymous phone call from a woman who asked, "Do you think it's right for you people to raise a cripple and still try to serve a church?"

This was after the trauma of Johnny's birth. It had taken months to get him out of the hospital and back to our house, which had needed some preparation. Neither of us had anticipated the impact this move would make on the church I was pastoring.

Before Chris got over the shock of that call, another woman phoned. "You know you could easily get someone to care for the child. But you live on sympathy. Well, don't expect sympathy from me!"

Then she received calls about me. "He's tearing up our church!" one voice shouted at Chris. Another said, "Oh, sure, he's filling the sanctuary—building up a bunch of supporters to stand with him against those of us who have been faithful all these years. Why don't you take that kid and get out of town?"

Chris went to the bedroom, closed the door, and asked God for grace to love these people who were making such abusive calls. Then she hurried downstairs and began preparing the best meal she had fixed in a year.

"Bon appétit!" she sang out when I entered the house.

I took one look at the table, spread for a king, and asked, "Whose birthday is it?"

Chris only smiled and hurried me off to wash up for dinner, and then we came to the table. We chatted and laughed together through the meal. Afterward, though, she turned serious.

"Something wrong?" I asked.

"There has been," she said. "But I want to help make things right." She told me about the telephone calls. "I didn't realize all you were going through," she said. "Why didn't you tell me?"

"And put a bigger load on your shoulders?"

"It will be easier for me if I know I'm sharing all your experiences. You want to know everything happening to Johnny, and he adores you for it. So do I."

We embraced. Beautifully.

We faced a challenging situation. I suppose if I'd had an eight-to-five job, things might have been a little easier. However, as I so often tell people on my staff, "I'm not looking for anyone who is seeking a forty-hour week but rather for anyone who is seeking a forty-hour day." The momentum of the ministry, if allowed to dissipate, would be hard to regain.

Nevertheless, to this day I stand in awe at Chris's ability to cope with the situation simply by arranging her mind the right way. She had a disabled son, an incredibly busy husband, and strangers making abusive phone calls. But she overcame it by God's grace and by sheer strength of mind.

The Power of Thinking

It doesn't take a clinical psychologist to tell you that the first thoughts you have upon awakening will affect the rest of your day. If you awaken with depressing thoughts, you will have a lousy day. If you awaken with positive and joyous thoughts, you will have a good day.

Abraham Lincoln said, "Most people are about as happy as

they make up their minds to be." Your thinking will bear fruit in your actions.

One of my habits is to make three new friends every week. I'm in my eighty-ninth year, so my gang is thinning out quickly! To make new friends, I need to contact younger people. This means I have to know how they think.

Another one of my goals is to have three new thoughts every week. (I don't want to die before I'm dead.) I write down these new thoughts and keep them for review. This has proven to be a valuable exercise. It sharpens my thinking and increases my memory capability.

In Psalm 1:2, the psalmist describes the godly man as one whose delight is in the law of the Lord and who meditates on His law day and night. So take just five minutes after you read your Bible and write down at least one great thought you derived from the reading. And then, as you have time throughout the day, recall that thought and meditate on it.

Also, watch where your mind is going during the day. We all talk to ourselves from the time we awaken until we go to bed at night. This self-talk can make or break you. It can forge a ball and chain to hold you in failure, anger, fear, and despair, or it can create wings and let you fly to the stratosphere of success.

I assume you have written out your goals with specific times for achievement. What could be better than to take time after your prayer and Bible study and meditation to review your goals and think about them? Visualize your goals as successfully achieved.

Put Your Subconscious on a Healthy Diet

One night when my father and I were having evening prayers, he shared a thought that has stuck with me. He said, "Lord, work Thou through our subconscious during the night hours so that our minds will honor Thee and fulfill our God-honoring desires."

When I was 17 years old, my mother gave me a book titled *The*

Power of Your Subconscious Mind. It made a positive impression on me then and continues to influence my thinking.

The wonderful thing about the subconscious is that it never sleeps. It works 24/7. It controls your heartbeat, your breathing, and most of your bodily functions whether you're awake or asleep.

Your subconscious has no conscience. It believes anything and everything you feed it from the conscious mind. So it's important that you feed your subconscious with thoughts that will enhance your life and, above all, honor God.

The late Sam Walton, founder of Walmart, said, "Expectation is everything."

The famous nineteenth-century preacher Charles Spurgeon said, "You might not always get what you want, but you will always get what you expect."

I recommend that anyone serious about maximizing his or her thought life read the book *Believe!* by Richard M. DeVos with Charles Paul Conn (Fleming H. Revell, 1975). From a Spartan beginning, DeVos and his partner, the late Jay Van Andel, built a global company that recently topped $10 billion in sales. It is privately held. Only the Lord knows what would be the market value of the company if it were to go public.

Your subconscious contains your entire belief system. That thought can be scary. Many times people have permitted into their belief system thoughts and ideas they would not want anyone to know about.

One day I heard a man lose his temper and blow up. To use the phrase of Winston Churchill, "He generated more antagonism than he could contain."

In just a few moments, he calmed down and said, "I didn't mean that."

My father quietly said to me later, "Of course he meant it. If he hadn't thought it, he wouldn't have said it." Jesus said, "Out of the abundance of the heart the mouth speaks" (Matthew 12:34).

How many friendships have been ruptured, marriages broken, jobs lost, and reputations sullied simply because damaging thoughts erupted in vicious words?

In the Bible we read, "God has not given us a spirit of fear, but of power and of love and of a sound mind" (2 Timothy 1:7). The words "sound mind" could be translated "self-control." Destructive thoughts issue from the absence of self-control. The verse also indicates that God doesn't give us a spirit of fear but of love and of power.

Job said, "The thing I greatly feared has come upon me, and what I dreaded has happened to me" (Job 3:25).

Put Your Imagination on the Right Diet

Keep your mind off the things you *don't* want and on the things you *do* want—assuming you want things that honor the Lord and thus profit you.

The imagination has a battle with the will. In each case, the imagination wins the battle. So don't say, "I don't want to do this," because in so doing, you are triggering the imagination. You focus on the very thing you're trying to get away from. Consequently, you'll move toward its enactment.

When I was a very young man, my father said, "Son, when you're confessing certain sins to the Lord, confess them quickly and move on. Otherwise, if you let your mind dwell on the sin you've been confessing, it will simply reproduce itself."

For instance, suppose that someone betrays me and causes great consternation and considerable personal cost. The Lord tells me I must forgive him. As a child of God, I want to forgive him. Nevertheless, while I'm confessing my sin of detesting him and asking the Lord to forgive me for it, I will only reproduce it if I keep dwelling on it in prayer.

If you've had some setbacks, focus your attention on where you want to go, not where you've been. Don't keep looking back unless you want to return there. You move in the direction of your thoughts.

You Can't Think One Way and Behave Another

You are deluding yourself if you suppose you can think one way and behave in another way. Your thoughts express themselves in your behavior.

The apostle Paul said to the Corinthians, "Evil company corrupts good habits" (1 Corinthians 15:33). Why is that? Because evil company infuses your mind with evil thoughts, and evil thoughts corrupt behavior.

You must work on your thought life continuously.

You wash your face and brush your hair a couple times a day. You shower or bathe once a day. Why? Because you know that deterioration results from ignoring these habits of hygiene. You don't look good. You don't smell good.

In the same way, if you're going to control your thought life and produce the kind of subconscious that embodies a productive belief system, you must practice daily mental hygiene.

During World War II, I was studying in Chicago and read an interesting story in the *Tribune*. Many young men were in the military service, so businesses had a difficult time filling leadership positions. One of the famous banks in Chicago had found a young man who seemed to fill the bill. The president of the bank was lunching one day with the chairman of the board at a nearby cafeteria.

The chairman said to the president, "I'm quite impressed with the bio you sent me on the young man you're considering."

Just then the president said, "Oh, there he is. He's in the cafeteria line."

The chairman looked and said, "He certainly cuts a fine figure, doesn't he? He looks clean cut and well groomed."

They watched him as he took his major dishes—meat, vegetables, salad. Then as he moved toward the checkout, they saw him take a small pat of butter and hide it in his mashed potatoes.

You can guess the rest. He lost the opportunity for the high-paying position. In fact, he lost the opportunity of ever being considered again by any bank for any position.

You might say, "For taking a pat of butter?" No, because he was a thief. The value of the stolen product had nothing to do with the character of the man. His thought life was defective, and it cost him a bright future.

Moses warned his people with the stunning words, "Be sure your sin will find you out" (Numbers 32:23). Solomon is just as clear: "As he thinks in his heart, so is he" (Proverbs 23:7). And in the New Testament, the apostle Paul emphasized the importance of our thoughts: "The weapons of our warfare are not carnal but mighty in God for pulling down strongholds, casting down arguments and every high thing that exalts itself against the knowledge of God, bringing every thought into captivity to the obedience of Christ" (2 Corinthians 10:4-5).

To be a success, you must engage in successful actions. To engage in successful actions, you must make successful thoughts the constant pattern of daily living. Don't cling to thoughts that do not conform to the life and teachings of the Lord Jesus Christ.

Over the 67 years of my ministry, I have often heard people say of someone who had sinned grievously—spiritually, socially, or even physically—"Oh, isn't it sad that he fell into sin?" But there is no such thing as "falling into sin." Any action is preceded by thoughts. When a person engages in behavior that ruins his reputation, destroys his family, and torpedoes a good position, you may know that a long period of mental decay preceded the visible act.

Jesus said, "Those things which proceed out of the mouth come from the heart, and they defile the man. For out of the heart proceed evil thoughts, murders, adulteries, fornications, thefts, false witness, blasphemies" (Matthew 15:18-19).

Take note of the company maintained by blasphemies, false witness, fornications, and adulteries. They share a room with murder! A man can engage in false witness, blasphemy, and adultery (provided it's not statutory rape) and maintain an enviable position in society. For murder, he will go to prison.

Are You a Good Self-Conversationalist?

When I was a little boy, my mother said to me, "John Edmund, you can have thoughts that I don't know anything about. Your father won't know about them, nor will your brothers. In fact, nobody will know about bad thoughts. However, if you entertain bad thoughts, and you do it repeatedly without confessing them to the Lord and repenting, those thoughts will inevitably put their seal on your face. As you get older, discerning people will say, 'There is an evil-thinking person.'"

That scared me in a way that I cannot describe. How often as an eight- or nine-year-old I'd look in the mirror and wonder if my thoughts had begun to show on my face!

Every disingenuous statement, every broken home, every ruptured relationship, every habit of employment nonperformance or poor performance...they all begin with defective thinking, with bad thoughts.

No wonder Paul emphasized the importance of casting down every argument and high thing that exalted itself against the knowledge of God. In your self-talk, you may want to use such statements as these:

- Thanks be to God; I feel terrific.

- I am rejoicing in the robust health the Lord gives me day by day.

- By God's grace and mustard-seed faith, I can accomplish the humanly impossible.

- I love my work, and I'm looking forward to a happy and productive day.

- Today and every day I'm moving closer to my God-inspired goals.

- He "who is able to do exceeding abundantly above all that we ask or think" won't let me fail.

- By His empowerment, I am already a success—and improving!

- As I persist by His strength, nothing can stop me.

- I am committed to do whatever is necessary to succeed.

- I'm joyful at this very moment.

- I forgive myself and others for mistakes of the past, and I put them all under the blood of Christ.

- God has made me unique in the entire world.

- By God's grace and strength, I can do it.

- My union with Jesus provides all the resources I need.

- I am almighty in the One who keeps pouring His power in me (Philippians 4:13).

- Today I will communicate with clarity and compassion for the glory of God.

When I was 18 years old and a freshman at Moody Bible Institute in Chicago, I needed some financial help. Fortunately, the Lord provided an opportunity for me to wash windows in a 16-story building. It was a good-paying job.

Each workday I reported to the reception desk and picked up the keys for the apartments I was to service. When I entered those apartments, I often saw degrading pictures, trappings of wickedness, and unspeakable pornography. This was new to my experience.

I remember praying, "Lord, I need this job. I need the money, but it's destroying my thought life, and I need help." The words of Philippians 4:8 came to mind:

> Finally, brethren, whatever things are true, whatever things are noble, whatever things are just, whatever things are pure, whatever things are lovely, whatever things are of good report, if there is any virtue and if there is anything praiseworthy—meditate on these things.

And then I thought of the chorus to the song "I Walk with the King":

> I walk with the King, hallelujah!
> I talk with the King, praise His name!
> No longer I roam, my soul faces home,
> I walk and I talk with the King.

So I developed a habit of opening the apartment doors without looking to the right or left. I concentrated my gaze on the nearest window, repeated out loud the words of Philippians 4:8, and then sang the chorus of "I Walk with the King." This may sound sophomoric to you, but let me tell you, it saved my thought life and permitted me to continue that good-paying job, which underwrote my expenses at school.

Win Over Worry

In 1959, I wrote a book titled *How to Win over Worry*. It has sold well over two million copies. It still sells, which lets me know that the book meets a felt need. It is more autobiographical than

I readily admit. I suffered a breakdown in my twenties. I used to get so depressed that it would have taken a jet airplane flying to its highest altitude for me to touch bottom.

Then I learned the lesson of proper thinking.

The personnel in my office have often remarked, "You don't ever get down, do you?"

I reply, "Thank God, no." I have not had a down day since the "conversion" of my thinking in 1960, when I was 36 years old.

Many Scriptures fortify my effort in this direction. And let me tell you, it's not a once-and-for-all victory. You need it day by day. Satan will do everything in his power to undermine your success. And he'll do it the most effectively and quickly by undermining your thought life.

"A merry heart does good, like medicine, but a broken spirit dries the bones" (Proverbs 17:22). "Be anxious for nothing, but in everything by prayer and supplication, with thanksgiving, let your requests be made known to God" (Philippians 4:6).

I like the insight and encouragement of the apostle Paul's words to the Romans: "Do not be conformed to this world, but be transformed by the renewing of your mind, that you may prove what is that good and acceptable and perfect will of God" (Romans 12:2).

Jeremiah 29:11 constantly encourages and fortifies my efforts in this direction: "I know the thoughts that I think toward you, says the LORD, thoughts of peace and not of evil, to give you a future and a hope."

Here are three more powerful passages:

- "Death and life are in the power of the tongue, and those who love it will eat its fruit" (Proverbs 18:21).

- "Either make the tree good and its fruit good, or else make the tree bad and its fruit bad; for a tree is known by its fruit. Brood of vipers! How can you, being evil, speak good things? For out of the abundance of the heart the mouth speaks. A good man out of the good treasure of his heart brings forth good things, and an evil man out of the evil treasure brings forth evil things. But I say to you that for every idle word men may speak, they will give account of it in the day of judgment. For by your words you will be justified, and by your words you will be condemned" (Matthew 12:33-37).

• "Keep your life free from love of money, and be content with what you have, for he has said, 'I will never leave you nor forsake you.' So we can confidently say, 'The Lord is my helper; I will not fear; what can man do to me?'" (Hebrews 13:5-6 ESV).

Space Your Repetitions

The worldwide success expert Paul J. Meyer coined an expression I want to impress upon you here: "spaced repetition."

We have all had the experience of reading a newspaper article that we find insightful. Usually, after a few days, we've completely forgotten it, which means we might as well not have read it in the first place.

It is the easiest thing in the world to write out a plan—and then stop. Writing a plan delivers a sense of satisfaction as though we had already achieved what we aimed for. But of course we have not. The plan is not an end in itself; it is merely a roadmap to help us go the right way. It is not the journey itself.

So reading about success and then ignoring what you have read will do little to help you in the long run. Instead, you should keep going back to what you have learned so you can relearn it and drum it into your mind.

That is spaced repetition—repeatedly focusing on specific steps you know you must take to achieve success. As the Bible says, it's "precept upon precept, line upon line…here a little, there a little."

The Argentinian pastor Juan Carlos Ortiz tells of arriving at a new church and preaching a sermon. The following Sunday he preached the same sermon again. On the Sunday after that, when he preached the same sermon for the third time, members of the congregation started to get restless. They asked him why he was preaching the same sermon again and again.

He replied: "When you put into action what I'm teaching you, I'll move on to something else!"

On another occasion, Ortiz told his congregation, "The message today is titled 'Love One Another.'" Then he got down from the pulpit and returned to his seat. There was a silence, and people started whispering to each other. Ortiz returned to the pulpit and said again, "The message for today is 'Love One Another.'" Again he sat down. After another pause, he did the same thing. "The message for today is 'Love one another,' and unless we start doing that, there won't be any more messages."

Juan Carlos Ortiz understood spaced repetition. He used it to good effect. What we hear or read repeatedly soon begins to stick in our minds.

Do you remember the first time you drove a car with a standard transmission? Do you remember when you stopped on a steep hill at a red light with a car in front of you and another car behind you?

You needed to start quickly enough to prevent the car behind you from rear-ending you, but not so vigorously as to bump the car in front. You probably took a few times to get familiar with the routine, but now you don't even think about the movements. You perform them subconsciously.

The same can be said of learning to play the piano or any other musical instrument. At first, you work consciously on every note. In the case of the piano, you watch the keys to make sure you are hitting the right ones. But the longer you go on playing the same piece of music, the less you need that feedback from your eyes, and the more your playing becomes automatic and subconscious. If you are a skilled pianist, you may not look at the keys at all.

Time to Decide

If you try to control your thoughts through willpower, you'll fail. When the imagination has a battle with the will, the imagination always wins. That's why the apostle Paul offers his example of "casting down arguments and every high thing that exalts itself against the knowledge of God."

The world says, "Accept who you are because you can't change it."

The Bible says, "Train your mind." Why? Because your mind is the track that determines which way your life runs. Ignore it, and your mind will take you in directions inconsistent with your deepest desires. Train it, and it will be your greatest single asset in your pursuit of success.

The world or the Bible—which are you going to listen to?

CHAPTER 12

The World Says "Relax"

The Bible Says "Treat Time like Gold"

IF YOU WANT AN INSTANT MEASURE of your success potential, spend a few minutes jotting down what you do all day.

Don't kid yourself. How many minutes do you devote to conversation, working, taking breaks, reading, showering, making calls, eating, watching TV, surfing the Internet, socializing with friends, playing with your children, talking to your partner?

Typically, most people's time management is like a molecule—small particles of real substance separated by large amounts of empty space. In other words, you can usually get a lot more into your day than you think you can. That's why the old adage says that if you want something done you should ask a busy person to do it. Busy people know about managing time.

Efficient time management is a science that anyone can master. But you have to be ready to do one thing—discipline yourself. If you don't discipline yourself, you'll be like an untrained dog, always running around off the leash, following your nose, unable to exert your efforts properly to a worthwhile end.

What Can You Replace?

Time is human life. When time runs out, your life runs out. The Bible refers to "redeeming the time" (Ephesians 5:16). To redeem time means to take advantage of opportunities for service. God has given each of us a limited amount of time on earth.

The New Testament Greek word for "redeem" could be translated, "secure for yourself or your own use." It can be rendered, "rescue from loss" or "use for a wise and sacred purpose."

Time is the only irreplaceable commodity. You cannot retrieve the minute that has just passed. It's gone, lost forever. So when you lose time, you lose a part of your life. When you have no more time, you have no more life. Your time is up.

Most other things in life *can* be replaced. You can replace money. My dear friend, the late Thomas F. Staley, lost everything in the 1929 crash. A short time thereafter a friend loaned him some money—I believe it was $50,000, which amounts to nearly $1 million in today's currency. Along with his young cousin, Richard S. Reynolds, he founded Reynolds Securities and died a very wealthy man in the 1970s. He restored his wealth, but he could not add to his time after the Lord took him home.

In many cases, health also can be replaced. At six months of age I contracted cholera. At three years of age I suffered near-fatal blood poisoning from bacterial contamination. At six years of age I came down with smallpox even though I had been vaccinated.

During my younger years I suffered all the children's diseases plus serious glandular problems. My doctor ordered me to stay in bed 14 hours a day, and I can still remember vividly the taste of cod liver oil, which I took in large quantities.

The day after Christmas 1940, I was riding on a back road with a friend in a Ford Model A convertible. We'd had a heavy freeze for several weeks, but then the sun came out. We didn't know about the ice under the gravel. Suddenly the car slid out of control and turned over. The windshield shattered and sliced my leg. Just a few inches more and it would have pierced my chest and killed me.

Streptococcus infected the gash in my leg. Thrombosis in my

hip was moving to my heart, and the doctors despaired of my survival.

"I think we'd better amputate," one doctor told my parents.

But my father was a man of dauntless faith. "Please wait just a bit longer," he told the doctor. He urged our friends to pray.

"I can't explain it," the physician, an avowed atheist, said a few days later, "unless, like you say, some power other than human intervened." All the same, I was laid up for nearly eight months.

Penicillin was unknown at the time of my accident, so I was given a large dosage of sulfanilamide. Conventional medical wisdom back then was that such large ingestions of sulfanilamide caused leukemia, which proved fatal within 25 years.

When I later took out my life insurance policies with National Life and Accident and Prudential, each company charged me a 25 percent penalty on my insurance premiums. They were convinced I would not live to age 40. (They later paid back the premiums!)

One of God's names in the Old Testament is Jehovah Rapha, "the Lord our Healer." He surely healed me. Now into my eighty-ninth year, God has blessed me with such robust health that Dr. Kenneth H. Cooper, majordomo of Cooper clinic in Dallas, Texas, told me in a letter, "You defy the odds." He thinks I may well be functioning at 100.

By God's grace and His miraculous healing, I regained my health. I did not regain the time spent in hospitals though. Because of laws God has put in place and cannot violate, even He cannot restore to me one day of the many years I suffered bed-confining sicknesses.

You Can Even Replace Lost Friends

Friends are not expendable; each friendship is unique. Nevertheless, lost friends can be replaced with new ones.

Paul the apostle wrote to Timothy, "At my first defense no one stood with me, but all forsook me" (2 Timothy 4:16). Ponder that! Many of them he had won to faith in Christ. And yet the whole crowd of them vanished when he needed them most. They turned their backs. Later, some returned, and new friends came on board.

Consider Jesus Himself. He suffered, bled, and died for our sins. Yet one of His disciples denied Him, one betrayed Him, and at the cross, "all the disciples forsook Him and fled" (Matthew 26:56). Since that time, millions have turned to Him—the "friend who sticks closer than a brother" (Proverbs 18:24).

But neither Paul nor his Savior, the Lord Jesus, could restore time.

The Need for Time Mastery

To squander your time is to waste your life. To master your time is to amplify your life. The apostle Paul's words to the Corinthians can be applied to every life: "The time is short" (1 Corinthians 7:29).

The nation of Turkey closed the Dardanelles to Allied shipping in the early days of World War I. The Allied powers wanted the strait open so that much-needed munitions could be sent to Russia by that route instead of through Archangel, a Russian port that was ice-locked most of the year. With the Dardanelles open, the Allied powers could unify their forces.

So in March of 1915, Great Britain tried to force the Dardanelles. The Turks sank three British battleships. The British despaired of victory and withdrew.

Intelligence later revealed the British could have opened the Dardanelles if they had kept up the bombardment for another 60 minutes. The Turks were out of ammunition when the British withdrew.

Only 60 more minutes and the Allies would have achieved victory. What a waste of money and lives just because the 60 minutes were turned to a misguided purpose. That one hour would have hastened Allied victory by months. Money would have been saved and lives would have been spared. In fact, the war might well have been won a whole two years before the Americans had to enter it in 1918.

Organize for Excellence

I met Hank McCamish in 1965. In late 1964, *Atlanta Magazine* wrote about him. It quoted one of Atlanta's leading businessmen as saying that Hank was the most self-organized man he had ever known.

That piqued my interest, and I determined to meet him. The meeting took place a few months later.

He stood six feet four, a handsome man with a charming manner. His office still gets my vote as the most impressive office I have visited, with its understated elegance and discreet presentation panels. As a mutual friend of ours, Phil Gordon, said, "Somehow I never believed that the man in this office would give you a raw deal." Phil is an astute and successful businessman and does not engage in verbal embroidery.

Hank McCamish became president of the insurance industry's Million Dollar Round Table before he was 40. I believe he has been a member of the elite Top of the Table since its inception.

One day, a group of his peers got together to discuss information retrieval. They knew they could go to a library and find anything they wanted, usually in minutes. Offices, though, were a different thing. Important information regularly got buried and lost. They decided to do some research and come up with an improved information retrieval program.

In time all of the other men fell away, but Hank was determined to find a solution. He spent a fortune on research and development and came up with the best retrieval system of its generation.

I recall a round-the-world trip with Hank and his wife,

Margaret, during which we stopped at Pan American's Clipper Club room in Tokyo's Narita Airport and had a two-hour discussion about organization. The *New York Times*, as I recall, had written him up under the heading, "Dixie boy shows Yanks how to do it." Hank recoils from publicity. On this occasion, he told me that the single greatest component of his achievement was organization.

How to Get Control of Your Time

You can't do everything, so you had better determine what you need to do to attain a life of achievement, happiness, and satisfaction. Some of this comes down to setting good habits.

President Franklin Delano Roosevelt always had a book at his desk. He read for the 10 or 15 minutes between appointments.

In the latter part of the eighteenth century and the early part of the nineteenth, British Admiral Lord Nelson attributed much of his success to the lifelong habit of always being present "a quarter of an hour aforehand."

Alan Lakein wrote the book *How to Get Control of your Time and Your Life.* It has sold more than 3 million copies. Former US president Bill Clinton started his autobiography, *My Life*, with a reference to the book.

Lakein says that planning and making choices are often hard work, to which I say a stentorian amen.

His simple priority system produces profound results. He says to write a list of tasks. Then place a capital letter *A* to the left of those items you think have high value, a *B* by those with medium value, and a *C* for those of low value.

To some extent you'll be guessing, but it's a move in the right direction. You optimize your effectiveness by directing most of your time first to the *A*s, saving the *B*s and *C*s for later. And if you want to get more detailed, you can break the *A*s into *A1, A2, A3,* and so on.

Lakein said you should resign yourself to not reaching the *C*s and perhaps not all of the *B*s. But that's the point. What you do get done is the part that's most important.

Had Lakein written the book today, I'm sure he would have recommended ThinkTQ, a program that applies his ideas to the digital age. It has certainly transformed my own vocational productivity. (TQ stands for Time Quotient. Visit www.thinktq .com/.)

TQ provides a gold-standard measurement of the actions you take to produce results over time. It measures how smart you *act*, not how smart you *are*. The program is based on 100 simple and easily repeatable actions and gives members a daily ten-minute power boost.

It includes one of the finest explanations of prioritizing I have read or heard. It also provides a numerical (and therefore unerringly accurate) score by which you can measure your performance level in each of the ten major sections of your life. Thousands of Haggai Institute graduates in scores of nations across the world use this program. Originators E.R. Haas and Kent Madson provide on a daily basis the finest personal development materials you will find anywhere.

Who's Running Your Timetable?

Nineteenth-century logician and theologian Richard Whately said, "Lose an hour in the morning, and you will be all day hunting for it." One way many people lose that hour is by going to their laptop and checking e-mail.

Personal development trainer Sid Savara says that is a very bad idea. "As soon as you get up, work on something important for 30-45 minutes, and only then check [your email]. If you can stand it, wait even longer. Some days I don't check e-mail at all until after lunch."

Why?

"By checking email, you risk doing what someone else wants you to do."

If you're checking e-mail early in the morning, says Savara, the chances are you haven't sorted out your own priorities.

"When you don't have a clear list of priorities, checking email becomes an urgent activity that you do at the expense of your important ones."

Also, "The more often you check email, the more often people will expect you to check it. Just stop checking it first thing in the morning and people won't expect it anymore."[1]

Never Start with Procrastination

Which of these do you do first—an important and enjoyable task, or a high-priority action, enjoyable or not.

Most people do the first before the second. They procrastinate by putting off tough decisions. They prioritize enjoyable tasks over high-priority actions.

Why do we procrastinate? I'm no psychologist, but I am a keen observer of human behavior. And I conclude we procrastinate when a high-priority action creates stress. Let me illustrate.

Shortly after six this morning I began writing this chapter. After nine hours, I had completed in final form about 2400 words. Then somehow I lost them. My IT guru said I had inadvertently closed the file without saving it. I was sick in the pit of my stomach.

Last night I had looked forward to an evening of relaxed diversion: a workout at the gym, calls to some friends, reading John Bunyan's autobiography, and working on my summer travel schedule. Those would have been far more pleasurable, but a deadline forces me to delay my normal bedtime routine and finish this chapter.

Of course, having to rush the job also adds the anxiety that I may not do it properly. I don't want to turn in second-rate work.

I don't want to invite criticism or disrespect by failing to give adequate time to a task.

My solution is simply to take Susan Jeffers's advice and "feel the fear and do it anyway." Nothing destroys anxiety faster than getting down to the job. As Emerson said, "Do the thing you fear the most, and the death of fear is certain." You gain strength, courage, and confidence by every experience of looking fear in the face and acting.

There are always a hundred and one reasons for *not* doing something. But if you refuse to take on the priority tasks simply because you are afraid they will turn out badly, you mismanage your time.

Suppose you do make a mistake. At least you have something you can work with. You can improve on something, but you can't improve on nothing. The late Charlie "Tremendous" Jones said, "Nobody can make right decisions all the time, but anybody can make decisions right." It's like a missile shot from a warship. It zigzags, but it continually corrects itself by responding to negative feedback.

And here is something important to remember. Finishing a high-priority task gives you a huge sense of achievement. One important decision made is one important decision you no longer have to be concerned about.

Negative Time

Some things take your time away. Interruptions can leave you feeling frustrated and unfulfilled at the end of a ten-hour day. You've put in the time, yet you feel as if you've accomplished nothing.

Strangely, we are just as apt to interrupt ourselves as to allow others to interrupt us.

Take the matter of e-mails. Dr. Gloria Mark, associate professor at the Donald Bren School of Information and Computer

Sciences at the University of California–Irvine, makes a startling statement: "From a cost-benefit point of view, in terms of worker time, e-mail does not pay off."[2]

During my last pastorate, I faced an epidemic of interruptions greater than I had experienced in previous pastorates. Some of my wonderful church members would arrive and say, "I wanted to drop by and have some fellowship with you." They would stay between a half hour and two hours.

I had to devise a plan to block interruptions without causing offense. The plan was simple. I removed every chair from my office except the one on which I sat. When people came in, I could stand, warmly greet them, offer a piece of candy and ask, "How can I help you today?"

If they had a legitimate problem, I could respond with help or I could refer them to the head of our counseling department, who was much better than I was at counseling. If they said, "I just came by to see how you are doing," I could thank them, have a brief prayer, and send them on their way rejoicing.

Very occasionally, if the need demanded it, I asked my secretary to bring in a chair. But it always went out again when the visit was over.

To my knowledge, no one was ever offended. God gave great growth. In 1954 the church registered more conversions and baptisms than any church in the 11 major denominations in America. As we said then, so I say now, "To God be the glory; great things He has done."

A detailed plan for the day and unswerving commitment to the day's priorities will neutralize the temptation to compromise with interruptions.

35 Time Wasters

More than forty years ago, Dr. Alec MacKenzie wrote a book called *The Time Trap: How to Get More Done in Less Time.* It is amazing how little has changed since 1970. Here is MacKenzie's list of time wasters.

Planning

- no objectives, priorities, or daily plan
- shifting priorities
- unfinished tasks
- firefighting and crisis management
- no deadlines and daydreaming
- attempting too much at one time and setting unrealistic time estimates

Organizing

- personal disorganization and a stacked desk
- duplication of effort
- confused areas of responsibility
- multiple bosses

Staffing

- untrained or inadequate staff
- too many or too few staff
- staff bringing problems into the workplace

Directing

- doing it myself
- too involved in routine details
- ineffective delegation

- lack of motivation
- no coordination or teamwork
- not managing conflict
- not coping with change

Controlling

- too much interruption by telephone/visitors
- incomplete information
- no standards or progress reports
- overcontrol
- mistakes and ineffective performance
- overlooking poor performance instead of correcting it
- inability to say no

Communicating

- too many meetings with too little purpose
- communicating too much, too little, or without clear purpose
- failure to listen
- socializing instead of working

Decision Making

- snap decisions
- indecision and procrastination
- wanting all the facts
- making decision by committee[3]

Understand 80 and 20

> Wilfried Fritz Pareto was an Italian engineer, sociologist, economist, political scientist and philosopher. He made several important contributions to economics, particularly in the study of income distribution and in the analysis of individuals' choices. [4]

Pareto observed in 1906 that 80 percent of the land in Italy was owned by 20 percent of the population. Time-management consultant Joseph M. Juran observed that the 80–20 proportionality cropped up in a number of places and named it the Pareto Principle. [5] Notice some examples:

- 80% of sales come from 20% of customers.
- 80% of production is from 20% of the product line.
- 80% of sick leave is taken by 20% of the employees.
- 80% of file usage involves 20% of the files.
- 80% of dinners repeat 20% of recipes.
- 80% of TV time is spent on 20% of the programs (those most popular with the family).
- 80% of reading time is spent on 20% of the pages in the newspaper (front page, sport page, editorials, columns, feature pages).
- 80% of telephone calls come from 20% of all callers.
- 80% of eating out is done in 20% of all restaurants.

This shows the importance of focusing on the *A* items on your to-do list. These are the 20 percent that deliver 80 percent of the desired results. If you have time, work on the *B* items—but only if you have time. However, the Pareto Principle reveals clearly why you should forget the *C* items.

In short, most people expend 80 percent of their time producing 20 percent of the results. So it's a no-brainer to determine where to find more time for productive work. Your timetable is already stuffed with unproductive time just begging to be reallocated.

Time to Decide

But a final warning. Some of the most successful things we do start off being new, untried, unknown, and uncertain. Doing them means taking a risk. They appear complex. They take effort. They carry the possibility of failure. They may involve cooperating with people you don't particularly get along with.

No wonder people give in to the temptation to sleep in the comfort zone of enjoyable, lower-priority tasks. It gives them the feeling they are accomplishing something even if they are accomplishing much less than they could.

So you must decide if you will compromise with mediocrity or daringly shoot for the stars. You must decide whether to obey the biblical mandate to redeem the time.

If you are a Christian, a child of God by faith in Jesus Christ, you may appreciate my life's motto. Tens of thousands of leaders and not a few churches have adopted it in more than 184 nations.

> Attempt Something So Great for God, It's Doomed to Failure Unless God Be in It.

The world says, "Relax. Life is too short to be struggling all the time. It's not the end of the world if you don't finish everything on your to-do list."

The Bible says, "Treat time like gold." You've only got so much of it, and God has a list of outstanding achievements that only you can accomplish.

The world or the Bible—which are you going to listen to?

CHAPTER 13

The World Says "It's Not Your Problem"
The Bible Says "Love"

Dr. E. Stanley Jones had just finished preaching to more than 100,000 people at the Maramon Convention in the state of Kerala in India. He had preached long, eloquently, and passionately about the power of *agape*. He expressed its meaning and distinguished it from the other words translated "love" in the New Testament.

After he had moved the minds and the emotions of the great throngs of people, he concluded by saying, "The greatest medicine for interpersonal problems is love."

On the way back to his quarters, a man who had heard him that night stopped him and asked, "What do you do with a person who continues to browbeat, bedevil, and even threaten you after you have shown every conceivable demonstration of love?"

Dr. Jones's reply reverberates in the corridors of my mind after many, many years. He simply said, "Increase the dosage."

You Don't Need Feelings

You will not find any reference to love in the Success and Personal Development sections of my personal library. Truth is, I don't remember ever having read anything substantive about love in any motivational books.

Yet love will put you higher on the ladder of success than any other personal attribute.

New Testament Greek uses different words to describe and define love. The most commonly used Greek word translated "love" in the New Testament is *agape*. This is God's love for us. It is an impartial, sacrificial love best exemplified by God saving us from our sin: "God so loved (*agape*) the world that He gave His only begotten Son, that whoever believes in Him should not perish but have eternal life" (John 3:16).

God gave His Son to save us from our sin—if we believe. He gave to us regardless of our character. His love is unconditional.

We don't give that way by nature. We usually give love in response to how we think people feel about us. Our love tends to respond to familiarity and direct interaction. The Greek word *phileo* defines that kind of love. In the New Testament it usually refers to brotherly love. *Phileo* derives from our emotions. Both believers and nonbelievers can experience this kind of love.

On the other hand, *agape* derives from a relationship with God through Jesus Christ because the nonregenerated soul is unable to love unconditionally. Agape love gives and sacrifices and expects nothing back in return.

Study the apostle Peter. His character was far from constant and God-honoring. Peter was enslaved by his emotions. He often acted before thinking, responding in improper ways. For instance, God had to interrupt him when he suggested building three tabernacles—one for Jesus, one for Moses, and one for Elijah—on the Mount of Transfiguration (Matthew 17:4-5).

Peter was proficient at expressing *phileo* and was probably popular because of his dynamic character. However, God wants us to express both *phileo* and *agape*.

In John 21:15-17 Jesus asks Peter, "Do you love Me more than these?"

Peter replies, "You know that I love you." Jesus asks him the same question again and gets the same response.

When Jesus asked him the third time, Peter said, "You know all things; You know that I love you."

Here's the story behind the story. The first two times, Jesus said, "Do you *agape* Me?" Peter replied, "You know that I *phileo* [I am fond of] You."

But the third time, Jesus said, "Do you *phileo* [Are you fond of] Me?" Peter was grieved (the meaning can also include sorrow) because Jesus came down to his level. Perhaps because Peter had denied Him three times, he didn't want to take a chance on again grieving the Lord.

Here's the point: *Phileo* is emotion; *agape* is an act of the will. Peter finally got the message and expressed it in his first epistle: "Since you have purified your souls in obeying the truth through the Spirit in sincere love [*phileo*] of the brethren, love [*agape*] one another fervently with a pure heart" (1 Peter 1:22).

Believers in the churches of Asia Minor had already expressed *phileo*, but Peter was encouraging them to fervently express *agape* as well. If you are a Christian, you are encouraged to express both kinds of love: the emotional love and the Spirit-led unconditional love.

In Peter's second epistle, he says that we are to behave with moral excellence. However, this is not enough. Nonbelievers tend to characterize Christians as those who tell other people how they ought to behave. However, the Christian life should not be restricted to just moral excellence, but above all else, should include both *phileo* and *agape*. Here are Peter's words in his second epistle:

> Giving all diligence, add to your faith virtue, to virtue knowledge, to knowledge self-control, to self-control perseverance, to perseverance godliness, to godliness brotherly kindness [*phileo*], and to brotherly kindness love [*agape*] (2 Peter 1:5-7).

They Read It at Weddings, but Do They Know What It Means?

The most famous chapter on *agape* is 1 Corinthians 13.

> Though I speak with the tongues of men and of angels, but have not love, I have become sounding brass or a clanging cymbal. And though I have the gift of prophecy, and understand all mysteries and all knowledge, and though I have all faith, so that I could remove mountains, but have not love, I am nothing. And though I bestow all my goods to feed the poor, and though I give my body to be burned, but have not love, it profits me nothing.
>
> Love suffers long and is kind; love does not envy; love does not parade itself, is not puffed up; does not behave rudely, does not seek its own, is not provoked, thinks no evil; does not rejoice in iniquity, but rejoices in the truth; bears all things, believes all things, hopes all things, endures all things.
>
> Love never fails. But whether there are prophecies, they will fail; whether there are tongues, they will cease; whether there is knowledge, it will vanish away. For we know in part and we prophesy in part. But when that which is perfect has come, then that which is in part will be done away.
>
> When I was a child, I spoke as a child, I understood as a child, I thought as a child; but when I became a man, I put away childish things. For now we see in a mirror, dimly, but then face to face. Now I know in part, but then I shall know just as I also am known.
>
> And now abide faith, hope, love, these three; but the greatest of these is love.

The apostle Paul here describes *agape* as being...

patient	believing
kind	hopeful
truthful	trusting
unselfish	enduring

It is not...

jealous	rude
boastful	selfish
arrogant	angry

True love never fails. The description perfectly fits God's love toward us and sets the standard for the way we should love Him and each other.

The Bible says that this unconditional love is more important than everything else (a partial list includes oratorical ability, prophecy, knowledge, faith, philanthropy, and hope). All of these good things will pass away. Only love is eternal.

Jesus said, "You shall love the LORD your God with all your heart, with all your soul, and with all your mind" (Matthew 22:37). He then added the second-most important law: "You shall love your neighbor as yourself." The entire law, He emphasized, hung from these two commandments.

If you attempt to exercise *agape* in your own strength, you will fail. This kind of love is only possible by relying on the power of God through faith in Jesus Christ. Even if you are a Christian, you will not succeed if you do not abide in Christ.

When I was writing a book on leadership, I spent many hours

perfecting a definition of *agape*. This is what I wrote: "*Agape* is the outgoing of the totality of your being to another in beneficence and help."

This love is not the exercise of the emotions; it's an act of the will. Let me say that again: Sacrificial love is not an emotion. It is an act of the will.

If you were to continually experience the emotional high you felt at your wedding, at the birth of your child, at an unexpected and huge raise in salary and perks...you couldn't handle it. Your psyche as well as your body could not sustain that type of fever pitch.

Agape, while often including this kind of emotion, far exceeds a temporary ecstasy. It's not a reaction to an outside stimulus. It is something you choose to do even if you don't feel like doing it.

Success Means Loving the Unlovable

When I was ten years old, I resented a kid at Camp Barakel in Michigan. He was the meanest kid I'd ever met and made things miserable for everybody.

My father, who served on staff as a counselor, would hush me up every time I blurted out my anger toward this kid.

One afternoon, Dad drove to Battle Creek, about 15 miles away, and I rode along. Just a few miles out, the car started sputtering. Dad said, "That's strange. Maybe the gas gauge is defective." So he got out and used a yardstick to determine that the tank was in fact empty. He said, "There's no gas, John Edmund." He had just filled up with gas before we left. Surely he could not have burned 15 gallons of gasoline in just a few miles.

He examined the gas tank and found a huge hole in the bottom. Someone had driven a spike into the tank. We both knew who was guilty, but Dad told me firmly, "Don't judge until you know the facts."

You cannot imagine the intensity of my fury. But I had an

old-country father and dared not express any opinions that might not be in line with his wishes. So I didn't say anything more.

We abandoned the Battle Creek trip and returned to the camp courtesy of a passing motorist who saw our plight.

Later that day, just before dinner, I was stunned and angry to see my Dad sitting on the end of the dock with that kid. To add to my fury, Dad had his arm around the kid as they talked. I later found out he was winning the boy to faith in Christ.

Now I guarantee you Dad did not like that kid. But he did love him. And that *agape* demonstrated itself in the outgoing of Dad's total being in beneficence and help to the little rascal.

Even the Best Excuses Mean Nothing

In 1960, I conducted a citywide evangelistic campaign in Wichita, Kansas. Afterward, somebody asked, "Was it a good meeting?"

I quipped, "Oh, yeah—it was on fire. The week after I left, the auditorium burned to the ground."

Seriously, the Lord had blessed the meetings with large crowds and many conversions. A couple of years after my meeting, the committee called to see if I could return for another citywide evangelistic campaign. I was booked solid, so I could not accept their invitation.

They said, "Would you recommend somebody?" I recommended a powerful evangelist who is now with the Lord.

They called me back and they said, "Do you know what he is saying about you?"

"Yes, I do," I said. "Unfortunately, unlike you and me, he doesn't realize what a perfectly wonderful person I am! But if he conducts the Wichita evangelistic campaign, I believe you will have a great meeting." And they did invite him and had a wonderful meeting.

I didn't like the guy and wouldn't walk across the street to spend time with him. But I loved him, and I knew he was a powerhouse for God.

Long-Term Love

Jesus said, "I say to you, love your enemies, bless those who curse you, do good to those who hate you, and pray for those who spitefully use you and persecute you" (Matthew 5:44).

You could hardly find a better description than that of Joseph's behavior toward his envious and murderous brothers. Right up to the end they were self-serving and deceitful. But Joseph, whom they had sold into slavery many years before, did not hesitate to treat them with *agape*.

> When Joseph's brothers saw that their father was dead, they said, "Perhaps Joseph will hate us, and may actually repay us for all the evil which we did to him." So they sent messengers to Joseph, saying, "Before your father died he commanded, saying, 'Thus you shall say to Joseph: "I beg you, please forgive the trespass of your brothers and their sin; for they did evil to you."'" Now, please, forgive the trespass of the servants of the God of your father." And Joseph wept when they spoke to him.
>
> Then his brothers also went and fell down before his face, and they said, "Behold, we are your servants."
>
> Joseph said to them, "Do not be afraid, for am I in the place of God? But as for you, you meant evil against me; but God meant it for good, in order to bring it about as it is this day, to save many people alive. Now therefore, do not be afraid; I will provide for you and your little ones." And he comforted them and spoke kindly to them (Genesis 50:15-21).

Joseph did not lack a case had he decided to fight it. Sold into slavery in Egypt, he was later thrown into prison for denying the attempted seduction of Potiphar's vile wife. Potiphar knew she was lying. If he believed she was telling the truth, he would have executed Joseph. To save the family reputation, he had to do something, so he threw Joseph in prison.

Later, Joseph correctly interpreted the dreams of two fellow prisoners, a butler and a baker. He said to the butler, "When you are freed, remember me."

As Joseph had predicted, the baker perished and the butler was freed. But he forgot Joseph—that is, until the king had a dream and needed someone to interpret it. Then the butler remembered and confessed his failure to help Joseph. He told Pharaoh about Joseph's miraculous ability.

After Joseph correctly interpreted Pharaoh's dream—something the court magicians and wise men could not do—Pharaoh not only released Joseph from prison but made him the number two man in all of Egypt! Is that success? I think so! You can read the entire thrilling episode in Genesis 40–41.

But you may say, that's a story from the Bible. Can we be sure that choosing to treat others with *agape* really works in the sometimes harsh and competitive world of modern business?

Put it to the test.

The Man Who Bargained the Price Up

The late Cecil Day, who built one of the largest budget luxury motel chains in history, practiced *agape* consistently.

On one occasion he wanted to buy a farm property. He approached the owner, who was sitting on the porch of his farmhouse. He asked the farmer if he would consider selling the property, and the farmer said he would.

Cecil then asked him what price he wanted, and the farmer gave him a price.

Cecil knew the property was worth much more and told the farmer so. He suggested that he have the property appraised. The farmer agreed and received many thousands of dollars more for his property because of Cecil's *agape*.

And Cecil, though hounded by financial complications created by the 1973–1974 recession, died a rich man. He gave millions to the Lord's work, including Haggai Institute. His widow, now Mrs. James Sanders, still does.

Mary Kay Ash has been lauded as America's greatest entrepreneur, providing well-compensating jobs for half a million women. She built a cosmetics empire, but she insisted her main goal and that of the company was to change lives. By example and precept she taught millions how to give and to live. A decade after she died, the foundation she established continues to assist in carrying out the *agape* lifestyle.

Similarly, the late John Wanamaker created the money-back guarantee that is now standard business practice. He gave his employees free medical care, education, recreational facilities, pensions, and profit-sharing plans before such benefits were considered standard. He also made early efforts to advance the welfare of African-Americans and Native Americans.

Johnny

In several places in this book I have referred to my son Johnny. Let me tell you a little more about the circumstances that led to his disablement.

The final stages of Chris's pregnancy were proceeding beautifully. One Sunday afternoon, as I got ready to leave for the evening service, Chris felt sure it was time to go to the hospital. I notified the hospital and placed a call to the doctor who had been looking after Chris from the beginning.

The doctor wasn't home.

"I've got to talk to him," I insisted. "It's my wife. She's ready for delivery. Tell me where I can get in touch with him."

The person couldn't help me, so we drove to the hospital anyway—a long haul from Lancaster to Columbia, South Carolina.

"Is our doctor here?" I asked as we pulled up to the emergency entrance and an orderly stepped out. But the doctor had not even made contact with the hospital.

"There should be no reason for alarm," a nurse assured us. "Patients routinely come to the hospital at the first sign of labor. Then the doctors arrive in ample time for the delivery."

"Will you keep the doctor informed?" I asked.

"Of course," she said.

But the doctor didn't check in with the hospital. Nor did any of my efforts to reach him by phone succeed. Just as I was about at the end of my wits, one of the nurses came in and said, "The doctor just called. We gave him a complete report, and he assured us everything was routine. He'll keep in touch with us."

"Keep in touch with us?" I fumed. "What kind of specialist is that? He should be here!"

Time dragged on. My wife became increasingly distressed. In the end we waited all night. In the morning I asked the nurse again if she had managed to locate the doctor.

"I don't quite understand it," she said. "I only got his receptionist. She told me the doctor was in his office, but was too busy to come to the hospital."

I exploded. It was incredible—absolutely and utterly incredible.

Later, the nurse came to the room and checked my wife's chart. She had been properly professional, skilled at handling the impatience of a first-time father. Now, however, I saw her register alarm.

My reaction to her alarm was to ask, "This doctor delivers babies here?"

"Of course," she said nervously, "several times a week."

"With this same kind of conduct?"

She stood mute, flustered. I hesitated a moment and bolted once again for a telephone. This time I got through to the specialist. Unbelievably, he was at a cocktail party.

He came to the hospital. But from the moment he walked into the room, I could tell he had been drinking. Nevertheless, I felt relieved. At least he was there.

"Let's take her into the delivery room," the specialist told the nurse. That same nurse subsequently told me that he should never have been permitted on the premises in his condition.

It was a breech birth with complications. Had the doctor been on hand and alert earlier, and had he been sober, he would surely have delivered the baby by a Caesarean section.

I waited impatiently outside the delivery room, pacing back and forth like a caged panther. Being a person of reasonable resourcefulness, I tend to put a lot of emphasis on problem solving. But here was a problem I could do nothing about at all.

The time dragged on. And on.

At last the doctor emerged. One look told me he was uneasy; things hadn't gone well.

It was ten o'clock the night of November 27, 1950.

"How's my wife?" I asked. "The baby?"

"Since you're a man of the cloth," he said, his head bobbing slightly, "I'll quote you something from Isaiah. 'He shall shave with a borrowed razor.'"

He gave me a sickly grin and walked out into the night, and I never saw him again.

What Does Love Really Mean?

The Old Testament misquote didn't make any sense to me then, and it doesn't now, not in that context. But when Johnny reached manhood, his circumstances were such he could never shave himself.

I subsequently learned that because of the doctor's delay and inept delivery, our baby suffered cerebral hemorrhages causing extensive brain damage. His jaw was badly injured. Both collarbones were broken. His right leg was pulled apart at the growing center.

"I'm willing to put my entire career on the line," the nurse supervisor later told me. "This is the most inexcusably bad delivery I've ever seen. If you want to sue for malpractice, I'll be your prime witness. Your doctor hardly knew what he was doing. To be completely frank, he was drunk. You might as well have called for an automobile mechanic."

Across my mind flashed the face of the specialist, the man who had robbed my son of his rightful beginning in life. Anger grew like a fire in my thoughts.

Then I remembered the counsels of my father, a giant in the faith among all the great men I have known. Quietly, but with strength and persuasion, he had challenged me to find God's sure will in this experience and to settle for nothing less.

I bowed my head. I don't remember the words I prayed. I know only that I dared to believe that my Lord was sovereign in the valley as well as on the mountaintop and that I could place my son with complete confidence in His care.

Can you understand the conflict I sensed at the prospect of a malpractice suit? Though I was advised to proceed with one, I couldn't bring myself to do it. This man was a craftsman, a brilliant, world-famed specialist. This was simply an exception. Suing him for malpractice wouldn't in any way help Johnny. On the other hand, I was sure that when he realized the tragedy he had created, it would sober him literally and figuratively.

In fact, it didn't. The same doctor went on to mishandle other deliveries, and he eventually died an early death. There's an argument for saying that by proceeding with a suit I could have prevented other tragedies. Perhaps that is so. But that was not apparent at the time. And that course of action could have opened the door to bitterness and revenge. I can honestly tell you I am glad that by God's grace, we passed that option by.

There were tremendous pressures, too, to abandon Johnny. The hospital medical authorities gave us an entirely bleak prognosis. "Put him in an institution," they advised. "What's the point tying yourselves down in your mid-twenties to the care of such an unfortunate little creature? He won't know the difference—whether *you* look after him or an institutional staff worker trained to cope with children in his condition."

What would have maximized my chances of "success"? Plenty of parents would have seen the logic of the hospital medical authorities. Your child's handicap becomes your own. Time that might have been devoted to Christian service and career building is instead eaten up by a grueling daily regimen of invalid care.

But of course, this forces us to ask what success really is. Success may be measured on the familiar and obvious scales of money, achievement, and influence, or it may not. In the end, the Bible says that success cannot be separated from the will of God. If God has thrown you a challenge, then as in Jonah's case, success lies in picking it up and running with it even if it throws all your expectations into disarray.

Suddenly Chris and I had a severely injured child. The chances were remote of his ever living a normal existence. Yet as I stood looking at our son (and I know it was the same with my wife), I had nothing like a sense of despair. Both Chris and I felt a total acceptance of Johnny. We wanted him. He was God's gift to us.

The suggestion that we should give him up for institutional care never took root in our minds for an instant. Johnny was our baby, flesh of our flesh. We wanted him even if he could only look up at us once a day, if he might just once gladden our hearts with a smile in all the weeks or months or, God allowing, years we would spend together.

Of the many lessons life has taught me, none stands out more than this. God allows no need in our lives for which He does not provide adequate supply. As others have said, our importunity becomes God's opportunity. It is a plain promise of Scripture. "My

God shall supply all your need according to His riches in glory by Christ Jesus" (Philippians 4:19).

In the book of Philippians, the apostle Paul stated that promise of God's supply after commenting on the Philippians' faithfulness in honoring God through their stewardship. Receiving from God is only part of a two-way street. We reciprocate by the outflow of ourselves, of our means, to Him.

Agape isn't sainthood. You don't need a special dispensation from God before you practice it. It's not something you need an aptitude for or something that requires a certain kind of qualification. It is just a way of living your life—a way that underlies every other principle in this book.

Time to Decide

Remember, *agape* is an act of the will. Anyone can display *agape* and profit from it. In business. In family life. Everywhere. You just have to decide to do it. It is God's greatest shortcut to success. It may look like the toughest shortcut you'll ever take, but it works.

The world says, "The world isn't perfect. It's a shame, but don't worry—in the end, it's not your problem."

The Bible simply says, "Love," because loving the Lord as yourself and loving your neighbor as yourself sums up everything that is required of you and every good that you could achieve. And you *can* change the world—if you have the vision and the drive to do it—because that's exactly what God wants you to do.

The world or the Bible—which are you going to listen to?

Thirteen Secrets and a Thirteen-Week Plan of Transformation

I GAVE MY FIRST LECTURE on success to a large audience of Christian leaders in Baltimore, Maryland in 1964. They responded so enthusiastically that I accepted subsequent requests to speak on the subject. After 48 years of similar audience responses, I decided to expand the material and put it in the book you have just read.

I commend the material in this book, not because I wrote it, but simply because I recorded what I have learned through Scripture, observation, and personal experience. And that has worked for me, as it has worked for thousands of others.

So what now?

At the start of this book, I asked if you were willing to be honest with yourself. I said that if you were not prepared to confront your weaknesses and deal with them, you might as well stop reading this book.

Well, you have read through 13 chapters, and now I have a second question for you: Are you prepared to act on what you have learned? If you don't act, any insights you have received from the Holy Spirit will inevitably fade away and leave you exactly where you were before.

A one-time read through will not correct a lifelong, habitual pattern of behavior that works against success. So if you're serious about living successfully, you must systematically and with discipline incorporate these principles into your daily life.

It's one thing to know what to do; it's quite another to do it. Let me illustrate.

My recognition vocabulary is far larger than my functional vocabulary. I recognize many more words than I use. If I want to improve my thinking, I need to constantly work on bringing more of my recognition vocabulary into my functional vocabulary. Why is that? Because words determine the scope, content, and penetration of my thoughts.

Just so, you may know all the truths about successful living, but your success depends on your routine application of these truths. Succeeding requires you to move from the recognition stage to the functional stage. You need more than knowledge if you expect to enjoy success to the full. You need to apply what you know.

The Thirteen-Week Plan

During my sophomore year of high school, my English teacher required our class to read *The Autobiography of Benjamin Franklin*. This book made an indelible impression upon me then as it does now, more than 73 years later.

Benjamin Franklin concluded that he needed to master 13 areas of his life. The number is a coincidence—the 13 areas he identified are not the same as the 13 secrets of success from the Bible I have just written about.

But his method has stayed with me. First of all, he set a goal of transforming his life and conducting it in a disciplined and scheduled way. Then he laid out a grid with 13 virtues listed on the left-hand column and the weeks 1 to 13 as column titles across the top.

Each week he focused on one virtue. In addition, every week, he graded himself on how well or how poorly he was doing with the other 12.

That's it. There was nothing sophisticated about it. He didn't need a complicated computer program to make it work—all he had was a pen and a notebook. Yet with this system, he was able to cover all 13 virtues every three months—that is, four times a year.

If I remember correctly, toward the end of his life he said he had mastered each of the virtues except order and organization—which is a paradox, since it is hard to imagine anything more orderly or organized than his system for internalizing his virtues.

What I'm suggesting here is a little less demanding than Benjamin Franklin's system. It is a simple 13-week program of personal change that keeps all 13 secrets of success under review at the same time. That is important because you will probably find some things easier than others. For example, you may have no problem setting goals but then fail to follow up because you don't cultivate support networks or maintain the habit of prayer. And it's no use taking a partial solution from the Bible. The 13 secrets of success are like a team—if you only send six players onto the field, you are likely to lose the match.

I suggest you proceed in two stages.

Stage 1: Action Steps

First, every element in the program of achieving success requires concrete steps, so begin by turning the 13 secrets of success into planned actions. You'll need some time to reflect on this. Don't rush it because everything that follows depends on expressing the Bible's secrets of success in meaningful actions.

Secret 1: GOALS

The Bible Says "Know Where You're Headed"

Write down your major life goal.

_____

_____

_____

_____

Secret 2: SUPPORT

The Bible Says "Attract a Winning Team"

Write down the names of three people who are instrumental in helping you achieve your life goal.

_____

_____

_____

_____

Secret 3: GROUNDING

The Bible Says "Check the GPS"

Write down three verses of Scripture that support your major life goal.

_____

_____

_____

_____

Secret 4: IMAGINATION

The Bible Says "Ditch the Word 'Impossible'"

Write down three barriers you will have to overcome in achieving your life goal.

_____

_____

_____

_____

Secret 5: LEARNING

The Bible Says "Never Waste a Failure"

Write down one failure you have experienced and what you have learned from it.

_____

_____

_____

_____

Secret 6: LEVERAGE

The Bible Says "Achieve and Build"

Write down one significant personal or professional achievement and how you are going to leverage it to achieve more.

_____

_____

_____

_____

Secret 7: PRAYER

The Bible Says "Before Everything, Pray"

Write down your reliable and regular plan for Bible study and prayer.

_____

_____

_____

_____

Secret 8: SIMPLICITY

The Bible Says "Keep It Simple"

Write down one thing you will do to simplify your life.

_____

_____

_____

Secret 9: CHARACTER

The Bible Says "Put Character Before Career"

Write down three aspects of character that you will remain true to in all circumstances.

_____

_____

_____

_____

Secret 10: GENEROSITY

The Bible Says "Give and Be Wealthy"

Write down a summary of your giving plan, including your tithe, the target, and amount above your tithe that you plan to give away.

_____

_____

_____

_____

Secret 11: FOCUS

The Bible Says "Train Your Mind"

Write down three affirmations you will repeat to yourself every day to help you achieve your major life goal.

_____

_____

_____

_____

Secret 12: TIME MANAGEMENT

The Bible Says "Treat Time like Gold"

Write down three ways in which you will improve your personal and professional time management.

_____

_____

_____

_____

Secret 13: LOVE

The Bible Says "Love"

Write down one new way in which you will show *agape* to others.

_____

_____

_____

_____

Stage 2: Progress Chart

The second stage will take you exactly 13 weeks.

The grid below is a progress chart. It lists the areas you are going to change and provides spaces for you to define exactly what actions you are going to take. It also provides spaces for you to score yourself in each area at the end of the week.

Here's how to use it. At the start of a new week (choose a time when you will be alone and free of distractions), write down the concrete step or steps you are going to take in each area during the coming week. In some cases you will simply maintain the same action you specified the week before. In others you may wish to choose new actions. Simply writing or rewriting these acts will act to focus your mind.

Take one step at a time. The first week deals only with the first secret of success. The next week focuses on the second and reviews the first. The third week focus on the third while reviewing the first and second…and so on.

In your weekly review/preview, score yourself in each area you have been working on. Give yourself three checks if you feel satisfied with your progress, two checks if there is room for improvement, and one check if you feel that particular area is not satisfactory or has slipped back. If you have given yourself less than three checks, record the reason for your lack of progress and decide how you will adjust your program going forward.

At the end of 13 weeks, you will have addressed all 13 secrets of success from the Bible and will probably have made a surprising amount of progress. From then on, it's up to you. If you wish, you can, like Benjamin Franklin, keep repeating the cycle until you feel you have sufficiently internalized everything.

Week 1: Goals

Success Secret	Action Steps	Score	Challenge	Fix
Goals				

Week 2: Support

Success Secret	Action Steps	Score	Challenge	Fix
Goals				
Support				

Week 3: Grounding

Success Secret	Action Steps	Score	Challenge	Fix
Goals				
Support				
Grounding				

Week 4: Imagination

Success Secret	Action Steps	Score	Challenge	Fix
Goals				
Support				
Grounding				
Imagination				

Week 5: Learning

Success Secret	Action Steps	Score	Challenge	Fix
Goals				
Support				
Grounding				
Imagination				
Learning				

Week 6: Leverage

Success Secret	Action Steps	Score	Challenge	Fix
Goals				
Support				
Grounding				

Success Secret	Action Steps	Score	Challenge	Fix
Imagination				
Learning				
Leverage				

Week 7: Prayer

Success Secret	Action Steps	Score	Challenge	Fix
Goals				
Support				
Grounding				
Imagination				

Success Secret	Action Steps	Score	Challenge	Fix
Learning				
Leverage				
Prayer				

Week 8: Simplicity

Success Secret	Action Steps	Score	Challenge	Fix
Goals				
Support				
Grounding				
Imagination				

Success Secret	Action Steps	Score	Challenge	Fix
Learning				
Leverage				
Prayer				
Simplicity				

Week 9: Character

Success Secret	Action Steps	Score	Challenge	Fix
Goals				
Support				
Grounding				
Imagination				

Success Secret	Action Steps	Score	Challenge	Fix
Learning				
Leverage				
Prayer				
Simplicity				
Character				

Week 10: Generosity

Success Secret	Action Steps	Score	Challenge	Fix
Goals				
Support				
Grounding				
Imagination				
Learning				

Success Secret	Action Steps	Score	Challenge	Fix
Leverage				
Prayer				
Simplicity				
Character				
Generosity				

Week 11: Focus

Success Secret	Action Steps	Score	Challenge	Fix
Goals				
Support				
Grounding				
Imagination				
Learning				
Leverage				

Success Secret	Action Steps	Score	Challenge	Fix
Prayer				
Simplicity				
Character				
Generosity				
Focus				

Week 12: Time Management

Success Secret	Action Steps	Score	Challenge	Fix
Goals				
Support				
Grounding				
Imagination				
Learning				
Leverage				

Success Secret	Action Steps	Score	Challenge	Fix
Prayer				
Simplicity				
Character				
Generosity				
Focus				
Time Management				

Week 13: Love

Success Secret	Action Steps	Score	Challenge	Fix
Goals				
Support				
Grounding				
Imagination				
Learning				
Leverage				

Success Secret	Action Steps	Score	Challenge	Fix
Prayer				
Simplicity				
Character				
Generosity				
Focus				
Time Management				
Love				

A Personal Note

I would enjoy hearing from you! Please feel free to ask me a question, discuss some facet of this subject more fully, or inquire about my other books, monographs, and recordings. The books cover many subjects, including investing your influence, mastering your money, and building relationships that will enhance your personal life and your career.

I pray that in reading this book and acting on what you have learned, you will find lifelong benefits and permanent encouragement.

founder@haggai-institute.com

www.haggai-institute.com

John Edmund Haggai
PO Box 13
Atlanta GA 30370
USA

About Dr. John Edmund Haggai

JOHN EDMUND HAGGAI, founder and president of Haggai Institute for Advanced Leadership Training, is an internationally acclaimed lecturer and leader of leaders. He is the author of several books, including *How to Win over Worry* and *365 Things Every Successful Leader Should Know*. He has helped people around the world with his practical formulas for winning over worry, pain, loneliness, and seemingly impossible situations.

NOTES

Why the Bible Holds the Secrets of Success

1. Richard V. Pierard, "The Man Who Gave the Bible to the Burmese," *Christian History & Biography* (Spring 2006) 90: 16-21. Cited in Wikipedia, q.v. "Adoniram Judson." en.wikipedia.org/wiki/Adoniram_Judson

2. Rosalie Hall Hunt, "Unforgettable," *Christian History & Biography* (Spring 2006) 90: 39-41. Cited in Wikipedia, q.v. "Adoniram Judson." en.wikipedia.org/wiki/Adoniram_Judson

3. Wikipedia, q.v. "Adoniram Judson." en.wikipedia.org/wiki/Adoniram_Judson

Chapter 1: The World Says "Don't Look Foolish"

1. Several paragraphs adapted from Wikipedia, q.v. "R.G. LeTourneau." en.wikipedia.org/wiki/R._G._LeTourneau

Chapter 2: The World Says "Rely on Yourself"

1. Napolean Hill, *The Law of Success* (New York: Tarcher, 2008), p. 5.

2. Ibid., p. 6.

3. B.C. Forbes, cited in Edward J. Wheeler, ed., *Current Opinion*, vol. 63 (July–December 1917), p. 309.

Chapter 3: The World Says "Grab Your Opportunities"

1. Silas Bent, *Justice Oliver Wendell Holmes* (Whitefish: Kessinger, 2008), p. 131.

2. Edward Bok, *The Americanization of Edward Bok* (New York: Cosimo Classics, 2005), p. 271.

Chapter 5: The World Says "Don't Mess Up"

1. J.K. Rowling, "The Fringe Benefits of Failure, and the Importance of Imagination." Cited in *Harvard Magazine*, June 5, 2008. harvardmagazine.com/2008/06/the-fringe-benefits-failure-the-importance-imagination/

Chapter 7: The World Says "Just Do It"

1. William Lyon Phelps, "Human Nature in the Bible," *The Ladies' Home Journal*, November 1921, p. 8.
2. Variously attributed.

Chapter 8: The World Says "Always Read the Fine Print"

1. Martin and Hilbert and Priscilla López, "The World's Technological Capacity to Store, Communicate, and Compute Information," *Science*, 332 (6025): 60-65. Cited in Wikipedia, s.v. "Exabyte." en.wikipedia.org/wiki/Exabyte
2. Ted Nicholas, "Biggest Contribution to Copyrighting," cited in *Copyrighter's Clearinghouse*, March 3, 2012.

Chapter 9: The World Says "Aim to Win"

1. "The Ethics of American Youth," Josephson Institute. charactercounts.org/programs/reportcard/
2. Cited in Raymond Loewy, *Never Leave Well Enough Alone* (Baltimore: Johns Hopkins University Press, 2002), p. 72.

Chapter 12: The World Says "Relax"

1. Sid Savara, "7 Reasons You Should Never Check Email First Thing in the Morning," *Personal Development Training with Sid Savara*. sidsavara.com/personal-development/do-not-check-email-in-the-morning
2. Jennifer Robison, "Too Many Interruptions at Work?" *Gallup Business Journal*. businessjournal.gallup.com/content/23146/too-many-interruptions-work.aspx
3. Alec MacKenzie, *The Time Trap: How to Get More Done in Less Time* (New York: McGraw Hill, 1970), n.p.
4. Wikipedia, q.v. Vilfredo Pareto. en.wikipedia.org/wiki/Vilfredo_Pareto
5. Wikipedia, q.v. Pareto Principle. en.wikipedia.org/wiki/Pareto_principle

Have you read Dr. Haggai's other excellent books from Harvest House Publishers?

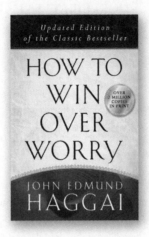

For 50 years people have turned to John Edmund Haggai's *How to Win over Worry* for practical answers and solutions. Now this classic bestseller on conquering worry (over 2 million in print in numerous languages) has been revised and updated for the unique challenges readers face today.

Dr. Haggai's compelling message on controlling worry presents biblical truths that can set you free, showing you how to...

- increase your financial security
- overcome the crippling misery of guilt
- maintain serenity in the midst of trouble
- improve your family life
- catch the habit of optimistic living

Real-life examples and biblical insights uncover the powerful tools God provides to break the bonds of anxiety and stress, providing you with a new way of thinking that will help you enjoy the peace God promises.

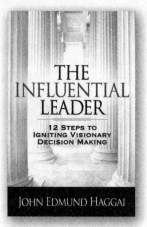

THE
INFLUENTIAL
LEADER
**12 STEPS TO
IGNITING VISIONARY
DECISION MAKING**

JOHN EDMUND HAGGAI

"I believe in John Edmund Haggai and am thrilled with the tremendous results I've seen in the lives of leaders."

—CHUCK COLSON
bestselling author, founder of Prison Fellowship

The Influential Leader is a powerful book on leadership from a visionary who has trained more than 86,000 people in 184 countries through the Haggai Institute.

Other books on leadership focus on *methods*, which unfortunately must keep changing as time goes on. But this book focuses on *characteristics* that are at the core of successful leadership and will endure no matter how times change.

Dr. Haggai's call to strong leadership looks at 12 characteristics for aspiring leaders, including...

humility	self-control
communication	opportunity
vision	staying power
goal setting	authority

You will learn how you can become a leader who influences people, inspires results, and accomplishes great things for God.

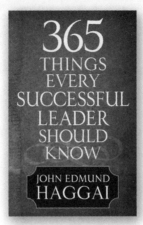

Renowned leader John Haggai has instructed many on the enduring characteristics and principles at the core of successful leadership. Now his leadership wisdom has been distilled in this collection of 365 pithy sayings sure to inspire and motivate you.

Here is just a sampling of the memorable daily reminders for all who seek to become even more effective in their leadership role.

> "Attempt something so great for God, it's doomed to failure unless God is in it." "The effective speaker has something worthy to say and says it worthily." "Leaders without vision are like guides without a map." "A large gift is a gift of any size into which the sacrificial spirit has been introduced."

This little book offers big inspiration for leaders and aspiring leaders in any vocation.

To learn more about books by Dr. John Edmund Haggai
or to read sample chapters, log on to our website:

www.harvesthousepublishers.com

HARVEST HOUSE PUBLISHERS
EUGENE, OREGON